Whispers to Heaven

Exploring Types of Prayer Through Biblical Examples

by Gary E. Risenhoover

TABLE OF CONTENTS

Preface

In the hush of early morning or the quiet depths of night, in moments of joy and in the shadows of despair, prayer breathes within the human soul like a sacred whisper reaching toward heaven. It is in these gentle, intimate conversations with the Divine that the heart finds its truest voice—sometimes trembling with awe, sometimes faltering with sorrow, yet always yearning for connection. Prayer is at once the simplest and the most profound dialogue imaginable: the meeting place where our earthly fragilities encounter the boundless grace of God. It is this mysterious and transformative nature of prayer that Whispers to Heaven seeks to unravel and illuminate, inviting you, dear reader, into a journey of discovery that traverses the ancient echoes of biblical testimony and the vibrant realities of modern spiritual life.

Prayer, often thought of as a fixed ritual or a mere recitation of formulas, is in truth a living, breathing expression of the human spirit's longing for union, understanding, and sustenance. Within the sacred pages of Scripture lie myriad types of prayer, each revealing different facets of this divine-human relationship—prayers of praise that uplift and magnify the sacred, prayers of thanksgiving that express boundless gratitude, prayers of lament that lay bare the wounds and cries of the brokenhearted, prayers of confession that unburden the soul with raw honesty, supplication and intercession that display our dependence on God for guidance, healing, and intervention. These were not mere words uttered in passing by the biblical figures whose stories have transcended time; they were vibrant, palpable outpourings of faith, struggle, hope, and transformation, imprinted upon history to guide and inspire.

In embarking on this contemplative exploration, Whispers to Heaven gently pulls you into the sacred tapestry woven by characters such as David—the shepherd king whose psalms soar from the depths of despair to the heights of ecstatic praise; Hannah, whose silent anguish transformed into a prayer of promise and surrender; Solomon, whose plea for wisdom echoes the universal quest for divine insight; Moses, whose interceding heart wrestled with the fate of an entire people; Jesus, whose prayers reveal the perfect communion between the Creator and the created, who models submission and intercession with exquisite vulnerability; and Mary, whose humble whisper became a resounding testament of faith and surrender. Each brings a unique voice to the choir of prayer, reminding us that our own whispers are part of a timeless, sacred symphony resonating from the dawn of creation to the present moment.

This book is not an academic tome relegated to the shelves of theological study but a warmly inviting companion for your own spiritual pilgrimage. It is crafted to be both a mirror reflecting the diverse patterns prayer may take, and a lamp casting light on the pathways to a deeper, more authentic prayer life. The approach here balances reverent theological reflection with accessible language and heartfelt warmth, aiming to nurture not only the mind enlightened by Scripture but also the soul stirred to heartfelt dialogue with God. Through guided reflections, vivid storytelling, and practical insights, each chapter beckons you to step beyond passive reading into active engagement—inviting you to pause, meditate, journal, and immerse yourself in the living art of prayer.

Importantly, Whispers to Heaven recognizes that prayer is not monolithic but wonderfully multifaceted, mirroring the complexity of human emotions and experiences. There is no single "right" way to pray; prayer is as varied as the individuals who whisper to heaven. Sometimes it will be a jubilant cry of praise brimming with light and hope; other times, a quiet lament steeped in sorrow and confusion. At moments, it will be a firm and honest confession, laying bare our shortcomings and seeking renewal. It might be the urgent plea in supplication or the humble intercession on behalf of another. And sometimes, prayer is simply sitting in stillness, open to the whispers of God's own heart. As this book guides you through these varied expressions, it encourages you to embrace not only the diversity of prayer found within the biblical narrative but also the rich textures of your own spiritual conversations—complex, authentic, and evolving.

In a world increasingly marked by noise, distraction, and hurriedness, the act of prayer offers a sanctuary—a sacred pause where time slows, where we are invited to listen and to speak in genuine vulnerability. Whispers to Heaven acknowledges the contemporary challenges that often cloud our spiritual focus, yet offers the hope that, by understanding and practicing the types of prayer revealed in Scripture, we may find renewed strength, solace, and direction. This book is a gentle call to reclaim prayer as a deeply personal and dynamic encounter—an evolving dance of faith and grace that invites us to move beyond rote repetition into vibrant life-giving dialogue.

As you embark upon these pages, may you be drawn into a deeper communion with God, discovering that prayer is not an obligation but a gift—a precious dialogue that meets us in every season of the soul. May the biblical voices intertwined here inspire your own whispers to heaven, shaping them into prayers that carry your spirit beyond mere words into a living conversation with the Divine. This sacred journey is extended to you not as a path to perfection, but as an invitation to authenticity and spiritual growth, a call to embrace the full spectrum of emotions, needs, and longings that prayer reveals.

So, with open heart and quiet anticipation, step gently into these chapters. Allow yourself to be moved, challenged, comforted, and renewed by the ancient prayers that still pulse with life. May Whispers to Heaven become for you a companion and guide, a beacon illuminating the vast landscape of prayer, encouraging you to find your own voice amid the multitude of faithful whispers spanning the ages. In doing so, may your communion with God be enriched, deepened, and continually transformed, nurturing a faith that speaks with courage, honesty, and boundless hope.

Foundations of Prayer: Understanding Sacred Dialogue

What is Prayer?

Prayer, in its most elemental form, is the sacred conversation between the human heart and the divine spirit. It is the echoing whisper that bridges the seemingly vast chasm between earthly frailty and heavenly majesty. To speak of prayer solely as words uttered in solemn moments or recited rituals reduces it to a mere formality; instead, prayer is the living thread that weaves the fabric of the believer's existence into the tapestry of God's eternal presence. Within the pages of scripture and the quiet recesses of countless souls, prayer emerges as the language of longing, the sanctuary of solace, and the furnace of transformation.

At its core, prayer is communication—an intimate dialogue between the finite and the infinite. Yet defining it simply as communication misses its profundity. It is an encounter that transcends the limits of human speech, a sacred exchange where words lift and hearts open, but where silence, too, often holds equal weight. Biblical narratives paint prayer not merely as the act of asking or thanking but as a posture—a turning of one's spirit toward God in openness, vulnerability, and trust. It is an initiation of a relationship that invites the divine to be present in every corner of existence, reshaping our understanding of reality and inviting us into God's embracing mystery.

The multifaceted purposes of prayer extend far beyond the initial notion of petitioning for divine favor or intervention. While supplication—the earnest plea for help—is undoubtedly a vital aspect, scripture illuminates prayer's diverse expressions: praise that magnifies the glory of God, thanksgiving that honors God's gracious gifts, confession that lays bare the conscience before a merciful judge, lament that voices the depths of human sorrow and anger, and intercession that lifts the burdens of others. Each form reveals a different facet of the human experience and a corresponding divine response woven through the biblical story. These varied dimensions remind us that prayer, like the life it seeks to sustain, is dynamic, evolving, and deeply textured.

The biblical writers frequently portray prayer as a spiritual posture—which is to say, a way of orienting oneself before God. This posture is one of humility and dependence, but also of boldness and intimacy. The Psalms, often called the prayer book of the Bible, pulse with this range—sometimes bold cries for justice, sometimes whispered songs of adoration, sometimes tears of repentance. Here we glimpse the paradox of prayer's character: it is both deeply personal and universally accessible, vulnerable yet courageous, human and yet touched by the divine breath. For example, David, who pours out his soul in the Psalms, embodies prayer as an authentic engagement with God amid the full spectrum of life's emotions. His prayers are not cloaked in pretense but flow raw and honest, inviting the reader to mirror such candor in their own sacred conversations.

Yet beyond emotional expression, prayer is undeniably transformative. The biblical record suggests that prayer changes the one who prays as much as it influences the divine response. Abraham's pleading over Sodom, Moses' intercession for the rebellious Israelites, Hannah's fervent petition for a child, and the persistent widow's demand for justice—all reveal how prayer shapes character, aligns human will with divine purposes, and opens space for grace to move powerfully in history and within the heart. These stories teach us that prayer is not a magical formula but a sacred dialogue mediated by faith, persistence, and surrender. Through prayer, believers are invited into a process of inner formation, wherein the divine word penetrates and renews, drawing prayers upward even as God moves downward in mercy.

Prayer also invites us into a rhythm—a sacred cadence that aligns human life with divine eternity. The Bible subtly reveals this pattern in its cycles of prayer—from the morning sacrifices of the temple to the quiet prayers of Mary at Nazareth, from the laments of exile to the petitions of Jesus in Gethsemane. Each moment of prayer invites the soul to slow, to listen, and to engage in a cosmic conversation that stretches beyond time and space. It is this rhythm that guards against prayer becoming mere duty or cliché and transforms it into a wellspring of spiritual vitality. Like breathing, prayer sustains the soul's life and reconnects the believer to the pulse of God's heart.

An essential element woven throughout biblical prayer is the posture of openness to God's will. The prayers of Jesus stand as the highest model for this approach—especially in moments of intense anguish and uncertainty. In Gethsemane, Jesus prays with raw honesty yet submits ultimately to the divine plan. This teaches that prayer is not an attempt to bend God to human desires but an invitation to align one's self with the greater will that governs creation. Such alignment does not negate human passion or petition but situates it within the broader landscape of faith and trust. This divine surrender becomes an act of love and courage, showing that true prayer is alive with hope and anchored in relationship rather than mere request.

Moreover, prayer embraces the whole person—mind, body, and spirit—inviting a communion that transcends the boundaries of intellectual assent or emotional expression alone. The biblical narrative challenges narrow understandings by emphasizing that prayer affects all facets of one's existence. When Moses ascends Mount Sinai, his prayerful meditation brings not only words but also physical manifestations of God's presence, such as the cloud and fire. The story of Elijah shows that prayer can culminate in profound encounters where the divine "still small voice" speaks to the interior depths of the soul. These incidents suggest that prayer cannot be divorced from the lived, embodied reality of faith. It is a holistic act that integrates the entire human being into sacred dialogue.

Central to understanding prayer is its rootedness in the biblical context of covenant relationship. Prayer does not occur in a vacuum but is embedded in the ongoing story of God's promises and faithfulness to creation and humanity. From Abraham through the prophets, the Psalms, and ultimately to Christ, prayer reflects this covenantal dynamic. It is the voice of a people invited to remember their identity as beloved children, to live in obedience and trust, and to seek restoration whenever that relationship is fractured. Thus, prayer becomes a vital means through which the believer participates in the unfolding drama of redemption. It is a liturgical act as well as a personal one, situated within the memory and hope of God's saving work.

At the same time, prayer acknowledges human limitations and the mystery of the divine transcendence. The Bible models forms of prayer that embrace silence and mystery just as much as words and petitions. The wisdom literature, for example, often points to the reverent fear of the Lord as the beginning of knowledge, suggesting that prayer is less about mastering God and more about cultivating awe and wonder. This sense of sacred mystery reverberates through the prayers of wisdom figures like Solomon, and it undergirds passages where God's ways are confessed as beyond human understanding. Prayer, therefore, is also an invitation into humble wonder, where the soul rests not in knowing but in reverent trust.

In contemporary spiritual practice, these biblical insights into prayer become a wellspring of guidance and inspiration. Prayer invites modern believers into a renewed encounter with the divine that respects the complexity of human emotion and the varying needs of the moment. It opens space for personal authenticity, allowing one to speak not only from a place of conceptual belief but from the rawness of life's joys and struggles. It challenges the tendency to reduce prayer to rote repetition or private negotiation, instead inviting a dynamic, living relationship that grows and changes. Prayer becomes a melody, shifting in tone and texture, shaped by the seasons of life, much as the biblical prayers collected over centuries reveal the manifold ways humans meet God.

Understanding prayer as communication with the divine also carries a profound implication: it places the believer within a community that spans time and space. The prayers of biblical figures do not merely exist as ancient relics but echo throughout history, uniting generations in a continuous dialogue with the sacred. When we pray, we join a chorus that includes Abraham and Sarah, Moses and Miriam, David and the prophets, Mary and the disciples, culminating in the witness of Christ himself. This communion of prayer transcends personal need—it is an act of solidarity and participation in the faith journey of the whole people of God. It is here that prayer takes on a social and transformative dimension, encouraging believers to intercede for others, to bear one another's burdens, and to live out a prayerful existence in community.

Ultimately, exploring what prayer truly encompasses invites a liberation from constricted views and a beckoning toward fuller spiritual maturity. It asks the reader to imagine prayer not merely as a spiritual task or religious duty but as the very breath of a living relationship with God. Through the biblical lens, prayer becomes an encounter marked by grace, vulnerability, and hope—a sacred rhythm that carries the believer through despair and joy, doubt and faith, silence and song. By embracing this expansive understanding, one cultivates a prayer life that is rich, varied, and deeply nourishing. It is not a monologue but a vibrant dialogue, where the soul's whispers rise heavenward and, in turn, receive the divine's gentle response.

Thus, as the foundation for this journey through the myriad types and textures of prayer in the Bible, it is essential to hold close the image of prayer as a sacred conversation—one that invites continual discovery, transformation, and communion. It calls every seeker to open their heart with courage and anticipation, knowing that every word, every silence, every lifted gaze is part of a holy liturgy unfolding between heaven and earth. Prayer, in its deepest sense, is the soul's abiding dialogue with the Eternal, the place where human longing meets divine embrace, and the whispered hopes grow strong enough to touch the very heart of heaven itself.

Biblical Perspectives on Prayer

From the dawn of sacred scripture, prayer emerges not merely as a ritualistic practice but as the very lifeblood of human-divine interaction, a timeless conduit that binds the finite to the infinite. Across the intricate tapestry of the Old and New Testaments, prayer reveals itself as a multifaceted expression of faith, trust, longing, and transformation—each thread woven with profound intentionality, inviting the believer into a sacred dialogue that transcends time, culture, and circumstance. In the Old Testament, prayer is deeply embedded within the lived experience of God's covenant people. It is neither a simplistic recitation nor a predictable formula; rather, it is the spiritual posture of a soul reaching upward, a heart attuned to the whisper of the Divine who holds both justice and mercy in His hands. The psalms offer a luminous window into this reality—rich with emotions that span the breadth of the human condition. From the jubilant shouts of praise to the anguished cries of lament, the psalmist teaches that prayer is honest speech before God, a sanctuary where even the most turbulent feelings find expression without fear of rejection. Here, prayer is not performed to manipulate divine favor but rather to cultivate an intimate relationship with the Creator, who listens and responds with tender understanding.

The Old Testament narrative further illustrates prayer as a dynamic, evolving relationship marked by dialogue and discovery. Patriarchs like Abraham intercede boldly, risking the precarious tension of pleading with God over the fate of cities, showcasing a courageous faith that confronts divine justice with heartfelt appeal. Moses exemplifies the role of the mediator whose frequent petitions reveal the intercessory power of prayer; he pleads for forgiveness and mercy on behalf of the wayward Israelites, embodying the profound hope and desperation embedded in communal prayer. The spiritual posture here is one of humility coupled with earnest expectation—an acknowledgment of God's sovereignty alongside a confident assertion that prayer can influence human events without undermining divine will. Such narratives teach that prayer is at once surrender and petition, a nuanced dance between acceptance and longing, woven through the fabric of covenantal trust.

Throughout the Old Testament, prayer encompasses an impressive variety—thanksgiving brimming with recognition of God's providence, confession that spills forth in brokenness and repentance, and lament that wrestles with suffering and injustice. These forms attest to the sacred authenticity with which biblical figures approached God, inviting readers to examine their own unfiltered emotions in dialogue with the divine. Prophetic voices, too, interlace prayer with calls to justice and righteousness, blending spiritual pleading with ethical exhortation. Thus, prayer emerges not as an isolated act but as a reflection of a life lived in alignment with divine purposes, where inward sincerity must ripple outward into concrete transformation.

The New Testament builds upon and deepens this rich heritage, unveiling prayer as the pathway into the heart of a God made manifest in Jesus Christ. Prayer is now illuminated by the incarnation, resurrection, and promise of the Spirit, transforming it into a joyful, even intimate exchange with the God who has traversed human frailty. Jesus models prayer both in its simplicity and its profound complexity, displaying a variety of prayerful postures: from solitary withdrawal in the quiet of dawn to intercession for his disciples and the world, from anguished cries in Gethsemane to exuberant praise. His prayers reveal an unparalleled transparency—his trust and submission to the Father's will coupled with his raw human vulnerability. Here, prayer becomes more than a sacred duty; it is the breath of divine life within the believer's soul. Jesus teaches His followers to approach God not with condemnation but with childlike reverence, embodied in the Lord's Prayer, which simultaneously embraces the holiness of God and the daily needs of humanity.

The epistles further refine this understanding, presenting prayer as a sustaining spiritual practice that intersects with all dimensions of

Christian living. Prayer is described as the means by which believers participate in the ongoing work of God's kingdom, interceding for others, seeking wisdom, and expressing a continual dependence on divine grace. The Apostle Paul's exhortations convey that prayer is integral to perseverance amidst trials, a channel of thanksgiving that transforms hearts, and a balm against despair and anxiety. This ongoing dialogue is more than transactional—prayer is portrayed as a transformative journey where the Spirit intercedes beyond human words, aligning the believer's will with God's perfect design. The New Testament also ushers in a more communal dimension of prayer, highlighting gatherings where the faithful unite in petition, praise, and proclamation, reinforcing the understanding that prayer both builds and strengthens the faith community.

Across both Testaments, the spiritual posture toward prayer is one of reverence, humility, and openness. Biblical prayer resists calculation or coercion; it embraces vulnerability as strength and seeks not to impose demands but to nurture a relationship. At its core, prayer is a sacred conversation marked by listening as much as speaking, a dynamic interplay where the human voice meets the divine whisper. The Scriptures present prayer as a living, breathing expression of the soul's deepest hopes and fears—a bridge spanning the chasm between mortal weakness and divine omnipotence. This sacred dialogue carries immense transformative power, capable of reshaping hearts, redirecting destinies, and revealing God's abiding presence in every circumstance.

Importantly, the Bible also emphasizes that prayer is more than a private act—it is profoundly ethical and communal. As seen in the prophet Daniel's supplications for the people, or Jesus' intercessory prayers for His disciples, prayer acts as a vital instrument in the spiritual fabric of community life, weaving individuals into a collective witness and responsibility. The ethical dimension ripples outward, reminding believers that effective prayer must be coupled with righteous living, justice, and love; the two cannot be disentangled. Prayer fuels action and empowers faith to move mountains, not as a magical incantation but as an authentic alignment with divine will and love.

Through its biblical perspectives, prayer is revealed as deeply relational—an invitation to enter the mystery of God's presence with the whole of one's being. It acknowledges human limitations yet asserts the possibility of divine encounter; it welcomes joy and sorrow, certainty and doubt. Such a rich presentation sets the stage for an expansive exploration of prayer's many forms and invites readers not only to learn about prayer but to live it, transcending ritual into a heartfelt communion that continues to whisper across the corridors of time. In preparing the heart for this journey, one is called to embrace prayer as a profound expression of faith that both reflects and shapes the soul, drawing the believer ever closer to the radiant light of God's steadfast love and mercy.

The Role of Prayer in Spiritual Life

Prayer, at its most profound level, is the sacred act of opening the heart and mind in sincere dialogue with the Divine. It transcends mere words or rituals; it is the precious, living thread that weaves the human spirit into the fabric of God's presence. Within this communion lies the fertile ground where faith takes root, character is refined, and the soul is nourished. To understand prayer solely as a set of repetitive phrases is to miss its vastness and transformative power. Prayer is the sacred breath of spiritual life—it draws us close to God not only in moments of need but in seasons of calm surrender, simmering joy, and humble adoration. The very posture of approaching God in prayer acknowledges a profound truth: that we are dependent creatures who seek communion with the Creator who sustains all things by the word of His power.

Throughout the biblical narrative, prayer emerges as the fundamental avenue through which humans engage the Divine Reality, a conduit of relational intimacy and dynamic interaction. The Old Testament is filled with examples—Moses standing face to face with God on Sinai, Hannah pouring out her anguish with silent desperation, David lifting acclamations or cries of lament from the depths of his heart. These portrayals reveal prayer as a multifaceted spiritual discipline, simultaneously an act of surrender and a declaration of trust. Prayer is not simply about asking or receiving; it is about aligning the human will, desires, and emotions with the divine will—a transformative process that invites the soul into participation with the sacred narrative of redemption.

When we explore prayer's impact on faith, it becomes clear that prayer is both a seed and a soil for spiritual growth. Faith without prayer is fragile and static; it is like a tree without water, unable to flourish or bear fruit.

Prayer nurtures the deepest beliefs, allowing them to breathe and expand within the heart. The Psalms echo this truth with vibrant intensity—the psalmist continually cries out to God in joy, fear, pain, and praise, each prayer cultivating a trust so robust that it withstands the storms of life. Through prayer, faith moves beyond mere intellectual assent to become an embodied experience of God's grace and presence. As believers persist in communion through prayer, their faith is often deepened by the tangible encounter with God's sustaining love and providence. This encounter nurtures a resilient hope, strengthening the believer to face uncertainties with a peaceful assurance rooted in divine fidelity.

Furthermore, prayer profoundly shapes character by cultivating virtues essential to spiritual maturity—humility, patience, gratitude, and compassion. In the practice of prayer, the ego is gently dismantled as the individual recognizes their utter dependence on God. Such an awareness humbles, fostering a heart posture that willingly submits to divine wisdom and sovereignty. The biblical example of Solomon is instructive here; his prayer in seeking wisdom above riches or power reflects a heart transformed by the awareness of human limitation and the need for divine guidance. This humble submission does not weaken but rather fortifies character, enabling believers to face life's challenges with integrity and grace. Likewise, prayer nurtures patience, as it often requires waiting upon the Lord in silence and expectancy. The believer learns to inhabit sacred stillness, trusting that God's timing and purposes are perfect even when the desired answers or relief seem delayed.

Gratitude, a fruit cultivated in prayer, shapes character by reorienting the soul away from entitlement and dissatisfaction to the joy of recognizing God's generosity in every circumstance. Biblical prayers of thanksgiving abound, such as those of Hannah or Daniel, exemplifying how consciously recounting God's past faithfulness nurtures a heart brimming with praise and hope. Compassion is also invariably deepened as prayer unveils the needs of others and the world, breaking through isolation into empathy. Intercessory prayer in particular widens the field of concern, inviting believers to adopt a posture of loving responsibility for their communities and beyond. Thus, prayer fosters a character that mirrors divine love, extending kindness and justice in tangible ways.

Central to the role of prayer in spiritual life is its power to cultivate an intimate and personal relationship with God. Prayer is not a monologue but a sacred dialogue, involving listening as well as speaking. The spiritual posture required for prayer—one of attentiveness, openness, and receptivity—invites believers into the mystery of God's presence. This relational dimension is beautifully illustrated in the New Testament, where Jesus models persistent, vulnerable prayer to the Father, embodying both submission and intercession. His prayers reveal the profound depths of divine-human communion, where the Son's heart aligns fully with the Father's will yet also expresses genuine human longing and anguish. In following this example, believers come to understand prayer as an ongoing conversation that weaves their lives into the eternal dance of love between Father, Son, and Spirit.

Moreover, the varieties of prayer depicted in scripture reveal the richness and complexity of this divine conversation. Prayer is not a uniform act but rather a symphony of voices—some tender and intimate, others passionate and pleading; some bursting forth in exuberant praise, others quieted in humble confession or sorrowful lament. This diversity reflects the fullness of human experience and emotions, affirming that God welcomes our honest and whole selves in prayer. As the book progresses, each specific type of prayer—praise, thanksgiving, confession, lament, intercession, supplication, and spiritual warfare—will be explored not only as historical practices but as living, breathing expressions accessible to contemporary believers. Understanding this spectrum prepares the reader to approach prayer not with rigidity or fear, but with freedom and creativity, recognizing that each prayer is a unique whisper rising toward heaven.

A particularly vital aspect of prayer's transformative role emerges from its capacity to bring internal healing and peace. When the psalmist confesses sins or pours out lament before God, these prayers enact a spiritual catharsis, releasing burdens and inviting restoration. The act of confession acknowledges brokenness and simultaneously embraces God's mercy, opening the door for renewal of spirit and realignment with divine grace. Lament prayers, often overlooked or undervalued, create sacred space for the honest grappling with pain, loss, and despair. In bringing these raw emotions into God's presence, believers find solace amid suffering and the hope that darkness is not the final word. These dimensions of prayer demonstrate how this sacred activity is integral to spiritual wholeness, touching body, mind, and soul.

Prayer also functions as an anchor in the turbulent seas of contemporary life. In a world increasingly marked by noise, distraction, and fractured attention, prayer re-centers the soul and recalibrates priorities. The quietude and stillness cultivated in prayer foster an inner sanctuary where God's voice can be heard above the clamoring chaos. This sacred pause replenishes spiritual energy and clarity, enabling believers to navigate life's complexities with wisdom and calm. Beyond individual benefit, prayer also knits believers into the wider community of faith, past and present, uniting whispers to heaven across generations. As countless voices in scripture and history have testified, prayer is a companionship—a shared journey marked by mutual encouragement and collective hope.

In sum, the role of prayer in spiritual life is both foundational and expansive. It is the breath of faith, the forge of character, the communion of the soul with its Maker. Prayer carries the believer from mere religious formality into a vibrant, ongoing relationship with God, nurturing transformation at every level. Through prayer, faith grows sturdy, character is refined by grace, and the believer is drawn more deeply into the love and mystery of God's presence. This sacred practice, richly textured and infinitely accessible, invites each reader to embrace a personal, heartfelt dialogue with God, a whisper that reaches heaven and transforms earth alike. As we prepare to explore the diverse forms and depths of prayer that scripture models, may this foundational understanding open hearts and awaken spirits to the profound journey toward the Divine that lies in every spoken word, silent breath, and whispered longing raised in prayer.

Prayer as Dialogue and Relationship

Prayer, in its richest and most profound form, is not merely a monologue uttered into the vast silence but is, rather, a sacred dialogue—an intimate, flowing exchange between the human heart and the divine presence. It is within this two-way conversation that prayer transcends ritual or routine, becoming a dynamic relationship where vulnerability meets grace, questions meet answers, and longing meets consolation. The biblical narrative breathes life into this dialogue, revealing prayer's essence as an invitation to enter into the very rhythm of God's heart, the pulsation of divine love and attentiveness. From the earliest pages of Scripture to the poignant prayers of Jesus and the apostles, we observe humanity reaching out across the chasms of time and experience, only to find God already present, ready to listen, to respond, to guide. This relationship, alive and evolving, reshapes not only the moments of speaking and listening but the interior landscapes of the soul itself.

In the evocative tapestry of Scripture, prayer appears not as a mechanical recitation but as a deeply relational act where the person praying comes face to face with the God who is both transcendent and immanent. Consider the story of Moses, standing amidst a burning bush, called to an impossible mission. Moses's prayer journey begins with wonder and hesitant questioning, an honest grappling with fear and inadequacy. It unfolds into a fearless dialogue where God's revelation calms Moses's doubts and commissions him with a sacred task. This early image of prayer captures the essence of relational engagement—prayer as both encounter and exchange, where the human voice carries not just requests but the yearning for understanding and connection. The divine response is not distant dictation but a guiding presence that holds the one praying within a covenantal embrace. Moses's interchanges with Yahweh teach us that prayer can be both a refuge and a clarifying force, a place where confusion turns into clarity through the patient unfolding of divine dialogue.

Throughout the Psalms, the heart's conversation with God takes on manifold expressions of emotional intimacy, showcasing prayer as a medium not only of praise but of profound honesty. David's outpourings reveal moments when speech soars in jubilant exaltation and others when it trembles with raw lamentation. In these prayers, we witness the fullness of human experience—the exalted joys of praise and the aching vulnerability of sorrow—woven seamlessly into the fabric of relationship. This reveals an essential truth: prayer, as dialogue, invites the whole person, not merely certain emotions deemed "appropriate." In confronting God with both cries of anguish and songs of gratitude, the petitioner acknowledges God's attentive presence as a loving companion ready to receive their unfettered truth. This interaction, marked by trust and boldness, underscores prayer's power to deepen spiritual communion, transforming the individual not only by the words spoken but by the very act of entering a mutual space of openness.

Yet, the relationship in prayer is not a static exchange; it is profoundly dynamic, marked by the ongoing movement of coming to know God and being known in return. Jesus himself offers the most profound model of prayer as intimate communion, especially through his own moments of withdrawal to solitary prayer and the intimate dialogues he shares with the Father. His prayers are not rehearsed formulas but heartfelt conversations filled with both submission and desire. They reveal a disciple's vulnerability alongside unshakable trust—a trust that redefines strength and power within the metaphor of surrender. When Jesus prays in Gethsemane, his anguish is laid bare before God in words that capture the tension of human will and divine purpose. Here, prayer as dialogue becomes a sacred theater of wrestling, where the human and divine wills intersect and where the very act of desiring alignment with God's plan becomes an act of profound relationship. The Gospels show Jesus continually inviting his followers into this relational prayer, offering a glimpse of fullness through intimacy with God.

The theological significance of prayer as dialogue ripples through the biblical understanding of covenant—an ancient promise that binds God and humanity in an ongoing relational bond marked by faithfulness and response. Prayer thus becomes the language of covenantal fidelity, a living testament to the reciprocal love between Creator and creature. This relational dimension infuses prayer with both freedom and responsibility. As the one praying learns to listen—not merely to speak—the relationship matures beyond initial petitions to a deepening of presence, patience, and trust. The Spirit, described in the New Testament as the divine Advocate, participates in this dialogue, empowering the believer's prayers and fostering a symphony of human longings and divine whispers that moves toward transformation. Prayer, then, is never a soliloquy of desperation but a mutual dance of grace whereby the human heart is drawn into deeper alignment with the eternal Love who continually seeks it.

Equally important to this two-way exchange is the posture and intention that the one praying adopts—an interior disposition grounded in faith and openness. The spiritual posture of the person praying mirrors the nature of the dialogue itself: one marked by humility, attentiveness, and receptivity rather than mere transactional recitation. Biblical prayers invite entry into this sacred stance, whether it be Hannah's fervent pleading from the depths of her sorrow or Mary's serene acceptance at the annunciation. These prayers reveal that relationship through prayer demands a vulnerability that risks honesty before God, relinquishing control, and embracing dependence. As such, dialogue in prayer becomes a crucible in which the ego is softened, enabling an authentic encounter with the divine Other. This openness is not passive but active, a willing surrender that paradoxically strengthens faith and trust even in the midst of unanswered questions or prolonged silence. The relational engagement of prayer is therefore a transformative journey in which spiritual posture sets the stage for a divine-human encounter and mutual revelation.

Moreover, the varieties of prayer—praise, thanksgiving, confession, lament, intercession, and supplication—each reveal different facets of this relational conversation. Each form is a distinctive voice in the dialogue, offering windows into the multiple ways human hearts reach out and God responds. Praise accentuates the recognition of God's character and goodness, a celebratory dialogue that rejoices in the divine presence. Thanksgiving fosters appreciation and acknowledgment of God's blessings, drawing the believer into gratitude-filled communion. Confession opens the heart in humility and repentance, creating space for forgiveness and renewal. Lament pours out sorrow and earnest pleading, trusting that God hears even the deepest pain. Intercession lifts others before the divine throne, expanding the relational circle beyond self to include communal need. Supplication embodies personal requests and needs, tenderly offered with faith that God listens and acts according to divine wisdom. Through these diverse prayer forms, the relational dialogue does not stagnate but continually adapts to the shifting seasons of human experience, inviting an authentic encounter with God in every circumstance.

This relational vision of prayer enriches our understanding by emphasizing that prayer is ongoing and organic. It is not confined to specific places, words, or rituals but breathes in the daily moments of life, inviting perpetual conversation with the divine. Biblical characters modeled this continual dialogue—Daniel's steadfast prayers despite exile, Nehemiah's whispered yearnings for his people's restoration, and Paul's exhortations to "pray without ceasing." These examples reveal prayer as a living thread that weaves through time and experience, ensuring that relationship with God endures beyond liturgical settings into the very fabric of existence. This constant conversation nurtures spiritual resilience and intimacy, grounding believers in the awareness that they are never truly alone, for God speaks even when human ears strain to hear.

Importantly, the transformative power of this dialogue lies not only in receiving answers or solutions but in the shifting of the one who prays. The relational conversation shapes identity, reshaping the person's understanding of self, their hopes, fears, and place in the world. The biblical witnesses testify to such transformations—Jacob wrestling with God emerges renamed and renewed, Peter's denial forgiven and restored through grace, and the prodigal son returns reconciled and embraced. In prayer as a relationship, God's steadfast presence meets human frailty, inviting a journey of healing and growth. This transformation is often subtle—an opening of the eyes or a softening of the heart—rather than dramatic revelation, emphasizing the enduring nature of divine love working patiently within the soul's depths.

In our contemporary world, marked by relentless noise and distraction, reclaiming prayer as dialogue beckons us to slow down and attune ourselves once more to the sacred whispers that transcend our scattered attention. It calls for cultivating a spiritual posture of listening as much as speaking, of sensing God's presence in the quiet spaces between words. Prayer as a relationship invites us to embrace not only the articulations of our desires but the silences that speak volumes, the pauses pregnant with divine intimacy. It beckons a return to the heart's vulnerability and the courage to dwell in the sacred mystery of God's attentive nearness. Such a practice teaches patience amid uncertainty, trust amid silence, and hope amid the complexities of life.

Ultimately, prayer as dialogue and relationship beckons the reader into a sacred space of mutual encounter where God's voice mingles with our own, where the boundaries between speaker and hearer blur in the radiance of divine love. It reminds us that prayer is not a burden to perform but a gift to receive and to share, a timeless conversation that unites the whispers of humanity with the eternal song of heaven. This intimate communion transforms not only the trajectory of moments in prayer but the whole compass of life, inviting us to move beyond isolation toward union with the God who listens, longs, and loves endlessly. In embracing prayer as dialogue, we enter into the heart of faith itself—a relationship vibrant and alive, rich with possibility and grace.

Praise: Celebrating God's Glory

Understanding Praise in Prayer

Praise in prayer is a profound and multi-dimensional expression of the human spirit reaching upward to acknowledge the glory, majesty, and unchanging nature of God. It transcends mere words, becoming a sacred outpouring that both reveals and shapes the soul's yearning to honor the divine. At its heart, praise is the adoration of God for who He is—His infinite holiness, sovereignty, wisdom, and love—and it forms an essential cornerstone in the architecture of spiritual worship. Unlike petition or confession, praise is not primarily concerned with what God can do for us or how we fall short; rather, it is an unreserved declaration of God's worthiness, a heartfelt response to His presence that lifts us beyond our circumstances into a realm of awed reverence and joy.

In the biblical tradition, praise is vividly illustrated through poetic literature, especially within the Psalms, which stand as a rich anthology of sacred songs that capture the depth and breadth of human emotion in communion with the divine. These psalms overflow with jubilant declarations, heartfelt affirmations, and passionate calls to worship, inviting readers to enter a spiritual experience that is both intimate and transcendent. Psalm 150, for example, culminates in a resounding summons: "Let everything that has breath praise the Lord." This verse not only underscores the universal call to praise but also elevates it as the natural, life-sustaining rhythm of existence itself. Praise is thus portrayed not as a perfunctory ritual but as the very essence of living in harmony with God, a divine dialogue punctuated by the song of the heart.

The emotional resonance of praise prayer is remarkable. As believers lift their voices or silently extol God, they move beyond mere cognition into an embodied celebration of God's attributes and deeds. The act of praising God opens the soul to an experience of joy and peace that surpasses understanding, a transcendent sweetness that reassures and strengthens regardless of external adversity. It is no surprise, therefore, that praise prayers often emerge in the context of deliverance and thanksgiving, where recognizing God's interventions rekindles faith and gratitude in the face of hardship. Yet praise is not confined to moments of triumph; it also serves as a steadfast anchor during trials, a spiritual posture that refuses despair by clinging to the certainty of God's eternal reign and unshakeable goodness. This dimension of praise reveals its vital role as a stabilizing force in the believer's journey, realigning the heart to divine reality amid life's shifting uncertainties.

The biblical psalmists demonstrate that praise encompasses both grand celebratory outbreaks and humble whispers of adoration. King David, a prolific psalmist, reminds us that praise is as much an internal posture as a public declaration. In quiet reflection or amidst the tumult of battle, David calls out to God, expressing reliance and reverence with honesty and depth. Likewise, the Song of Hannah expresses praise borne out of personal longing fulfilled, a tender yet powerful acknowledgment of God's providence that emerges from the depths of human vulnerability. This breadth illustrates that praise is not limited to ecstatic joy but also embraces contemplative thanksgiving and the sober acknowledgment of God's righteous character. The varied expressions of praise captured in scripture thus encourage believers to engage in a prayer form that is both dynamic and deeply personal, inviting them to articulate their unique relationship with God in ways that resonate authentically within their experience.

Spiritually, praise operates as a transformative dialogue in which the worshiper acknowledges God's holiness while simultaneously opening themselves to divine grace. It is a humbling act that recognizes human limitation but also elevates the believer by orienting the soul toward divine transcendence. Theologians have long noted that praise reveals the reciprocal nature of prayer: while God is the eternal subject of worship, the act of praising God changes the worshiper. The soul that praises aligns itself more closely to divine will, shedding selfish concerns and opening to a broader vision of reality imbued with sacred meaning. Through praise, the believer is drawn into a sacred rhythm that mirrors the celestial harmony, participating in the eternal chorus of heaven itself. This spiritual journey, marked by praise, thus nurtures growth, healing, and a heightened awareness of God's omnipresent majesty.

Moreover, praise prayer in the Bible frequently serves as a communal act, binding the faithful in shared recognition of God's greatness. The collective singing of psalms and hymns not only reinforces theological truths but also strengthens the bonds of community through unified worship. The shared experience of lifting voices in praise cultivates spiritual solidarity and mutual encouragement, reminding believers that they are part of a larger, timeless fellowship that transcends generations and geographies. This communal aspect of praise has practical implications for contemporary worship, where collective praise continues to play a vital role in nurturing faith and fostering a sense of belonging among believers. In recognizing praise as both personal and communal, biblical tradition offers a model for believers to engage in worship that is holistic, encompassing individual devotion and broader ecclesial participation.

The language of praise in biblical prayers is rich with imagery, metaphor, and poetic devices that evoke the grandeur of creation and God's rightful place as its sovereign ruler. The psalmists frequently employ vivid depictions of nature—the heavens declared as God's handiwork, mountains rejoicing, oceans roaring—to communicate the universal scope of God's glory. This poetic language invites readers to perceive praise not only as a verbal articulation but also as a sensory and imaginative experience that connects the worshiper with the vastness of God's creative power. Such imagery helps to stir the affections and elevate the heart, making praise an experience that touches every facet of human existence. Through this symbolic language, praise becomes a bridge linking earthly realities with the divine realm, drawing believers into a space where the material and spiritual intersect in worshipful awe.

Theologically, praise underscores God's intrinsic worthiness, independent of human actions or circumstances. Unlike supplication, where the petitioner seeks divine intervention, praise focuses on God's eternal nature—the God who is, was, and will be. This emphasis affirms that God's majesty stands apart from—and prior to—any human need or response. Praise thus communicates a profound truth at the heart of biblical faith: God's identity and glory are not contingent upon human acknowledgment, but rather human beings find their true purpose and fulfillment in recognizing and joining in that glory. This orientation challenges believers to move beyond transactional notions of prayer into a posture of awe and surrender, acknowledging God as the source and sustainer of all life and blessing.

Such recognition calls forth a spirit of gratitude embedded within praise. To praise God is to acknowledge the manifold ways God's faithfulness permeates human history and personal experience. The biblical record abounds with evidence of God's steadfast love, justice, mercy, and power—each a reason to lift the soul in praise. This awareness of God's active presence inspires the believer to respond with unrestrained gratitude, transforming prayer into a space of joyous encounter where the heart speaks in thankfulness as well as adoration. Praise and thanksgiving thus coexist intimately; while praise acknowledges God's character and being, thanksgiving celebrates God's actions, creating a rich texture of worship that nourishes and sustains the spiritual life.

In the life of Jesus, praise prayer also takes on profound significance. Although often depicted praying in solitude with petitions and intercession, Jesus models praise through his acknowledgments of the Father's holiness and goodness. His hymn at the Last Supper and his moments of lifting eyes heavenward illustrate that praise remains central even amid the weightiest moments of human experience. Jesus embodies the perfect harmony of praise—offered not only in joyful exaltation but also in steadfast trust and submission—reminding believers that praise is a form of spiritual strength and resilience amid trials. His example calls the faithful to embrace praise not as an optional adornment of prayer life but as a vital means of aligning the heart to God's presence at all times.

Practically speaking, cultivating praise in one's own prayer life involves intentionality and openness. The ancient biblical prayers teach that praise need not be confined to formulaic expressions but can be heartfelt and spontaneous, arising from the nuances of daily life and personal reflection. Encouraging believers to meditate on God's attributes, recall moments of deliverance, and contemplate the beauty and order of creation provides fertile ground for praise to blossom. Furthermore, praising God in community—through song, spoken word, or silent awe—can deepen one's experience of the sacred and foster a pervasive sense of joy and peace. Engaging the imagination with scriptural metaphors or poetry also enriches praise, transforming it into a vibrant, living encounter with the divine.

Ultimately, the role of praise in spiritual worship is to draw the believer into a closer, more intimate connection with God. It orients the heart toward the eternal and the holy, inviting a transformation of perspective that relocates human concerns within the vastness of divine love. Praise awakens the soul to the continuous presence of God in the rhythms of life, enabling the worshiper to transcend isolation and despair through a communion that rejoices in the steadfastness of God's nature. This sacred dialogue, captured in the biblical narratives and echoed in the daily prayers of countless believers, remains an enduring wellspring of spiritual vitality, nourishing faith and illuminating the path toward deeper devotion. Through praise, the whispers of the human heart rise like incense, ascending to heaven in sacred harmony with the eternal song of the cosmos, forever honoring the God who reigns in majesty and mercy.

Praising God Through the Psalms

The Psalms stand as a towering testament to the profound human capacity to elevate the soul through praise, capturing in their poetic brilliance the vast spectrum of emotions and declarations that arise when hearts turn heavenward in adoration. To immerse oneself in the Psalms is to enter a sanctuary of sound and spirit, where words dance with melody and meaning, crafting a language of worship infused with reverence, joy, awe, and unshakable faith. These sacred songs reveal praise not merely as an act of verbal homage but as an all-encompassing experience—an outpouring of gratitude and wonder that reaches beyond mere words into the realms of the heart and spirit. They encapsulate the believer's yearning to acknowledge God's greatness, the intricate beauty of creation, and the unchanging faithfulness that sustains life through every storm.

In many psalms, praise blossoms in radiant imagery, evocative metaphors, and tightly woven parallelism, a hallmark of Hebrew poetry that intensifies the emotional resonance of each declaration. Consider the majestic unfolding of Psalm 8, where the psalmist contemplates the heavens' splendor, the moon and stars set in their courses, and marvels at the seeming paradox of a God so vast who yet has bestowed dignity upon humankind. The repetition and balanced pairs of phrases—"What is man that you are mindful of him?"—linger in the air like a sacred breath, inviting the worshiper into intimate reflection on divine care. Here, praise becomes a recognition of God's meticulous artistry in creation, a deeply personal awe that fuels the soul's upward longing. Such poetic structure does more than ornament the text; it mirrors the rhythmic flow of worship itself, where exaltation rises and falls like a sacred chant, drawing the worshiper ever closer to the presence of divine majesty.

Psalm 145 offers another luminous example, often called the "Great Praise Psalm," which cascades through an alphabetical progression that seems designed to encompass the totality of creation and existence in its adulation. Each line calls forth a new facet of God's character—His compassion, righteousness, might, and eternal reign—unfolding as a celestial tapestry woven with words. The psalmist does not simply state these truths but sings them in language that brims with vitality and confidence. The repetition of "Great is the Lord and greatly to be praised" functions as a liturgical refrain, embedding in the believer's consciousness an unshakeable conviction of God's supreme worthiness. This refrain, appearing as a rhythmic heartbeat in the psalm, offers a spiritual anchor, instilling a sense of security and joyous devotion that enriches the worship experience and encourages communal participation.

The emotional texture of praise in the Psalms often intertwines with expressions of gratitude and delight, forming a chorus that resonates deeply within human experience. Psalm 100 captures this exuberance with its jubilant call: "Make a joyful noise to the Lord, all the earth! Serve the Lord with gladness! Come into his presence with singing!" The sheer vitality of these imperatives propels the reader into an active posture of worship, rejoicing in God's goodness embodied as "His steadfast love endures forever." The poetry here is effusive, candid, and electrifying—almost contagious in its cheer—lending itself to public celebration and private meditation alike. This psalm, with its simplicity and universal appeal, reminds readers that praise is not reserved for solemn moments but is a living, breathing act of joy that colors everyday life with hope and spiritual buoyancy.

Yet, beyond their celebration, the Psalms articulate praise as a deeply relational act, acknowledging not only God's cosmic power but His personal faithfulness. Psalm 103 exemplifies this intimate dimension, as the psalmist exhorts the heart to "Bless the Lord, O my soul, and all that is within me, bless his holy name!" The structure of the psalm gradually unveils the mercies of God: forgiveness, healing, redemption, and tender compassion. The poetic flow here suggests a dynamic movement from recognition of divine grandeur to the warmth of God's tender love, highlighting that true praise is not distant awe but a heartfelt response to God's covenantal kindness. The psalm's cadence, alternating between solemn declaration and tender recollection, mirrors the complexity of worship, inviting believers to recognize God's power expressed through mercy as the foundation of heartfelt adoration.

Echoing through these texts is the profound awareness of God's sovereignty and timelessness that elevates praise beyond the temporal. Psalm 93, brief yet potent, rings with regal authority, affirming, "The Lord reigns; he is robed in majesty; the Lord is robed; he has put on strength as his belt." The imagery evokes the grandeur of a king arrayed in royal garments, conjuring awe and submission. This psalm captures a moment of cosmic order, where the tumultuous forces of chaos are subdued under divine rule. The poetic elements here—metaphor, repetition, and vivid sensory detail—create an atmosphere in which praise is an act of recognition and surrender to an unchanging, powerful God whose throne is eternal. This portrayal offers a spiritual refuge, reminding worshipers that, amid life's uncertainties, the divine reign is steadfast and noble.

Within the psalmic tradition, the language of praise is often enriched by the musicality intrinsic to Hebrew poetry, employing parallelism and imagery that lend themselves naturally to song and chant. This musicality is not merely decorative but serves as a conduit for deeper spiritual engagement, allowing the rhythmic repetition and poetic balance to embed praise within the worshiper's mind and heart. The interplay of synonymous and antithetic parallelism intensifies the message, creating layers of meaning that invite contemplation and emotional participation. The poetic form mirrors the spiritual rhythm of praise itself: a cycle of exaltation, reflection, and adoration that lifts the soul in a harmonious dance with the divine. It is in this sacred space that the psalms transform simple words into a vessel for profound spiritual experience.

Some psalms also weave praise with the acknowledgment of God's enduring faithfulness in times of personal trial, reinforcing the connection between praise and trust. Psalm 34, for instance, begins with delight and praise for deliverance while also recounting God's attentive care amid distress. This juxtaposition of joy and struggle underscores praise as an act of resilience and hope, rooted not in circumstance but in the steadfast love of God. The poetic narrative moves fluidly between exultant acclaim and humble testimony, inviting readers to recognize that praise nurtures spiritual endurance by reminding the heart of God's unchanging presence. The psalmist's vivid descriptions of God as "close to the brokenhearted" and "saves those who are crushed in spirit" enliven praise as a deeply personal and healing encounter, making it a powerful source of comfort and strength.

Turning to the New Testament, while the Psalms form the cornerstone of biblical praise, expressions of adoration continue to resonate through the prayers and hymns surrounding the life of Jesus and the early church. Yet, the Psalms remain unparalleled in their poetic craft and emotional depth, providing a wellspring from which Christian communities have drawn for millennia. Their language shapes the vocabulary of praise, offering a spiritual lexicon that blends loftiness with intimacy, grandeur with vulnerability. The consistent thread is an invitation to recognize God's transcendent majesty while embracing the tender nearness that invites personal communion. In this way, the Psalms offer believers a template for elevating their own prayers beyond routine, infusing them with the freshness and fervor found in sacred poetry.

Embracing these psalmic praises in contemporary prayer life calls for engaging the text not only as scripture to be studied but as a living dialogue that stirs the soul. By vocalizing or meditating on passages such as those exalted in Psalms 8, 100, 145, and 103, believers open themselves to a transcendent conversation where praise rises spontaneously, fed by the beauty, mercy, and grandeur witnessed in every facet of existence. The poetic forms themselves serve as invitations to linger in contemplation— to savor the balance, the echo, and the resonance of each phrase like a sacred melody. In this quiet engagement, praise becomes less an obligation and more a blossoming of the spirit, a heartfelt response to the divine presence that permeates all life.

Moreover, the Psalms demonstrate that praise is not a static or one-dimensional exercise but a vibrant, evolving expression that encompasses joy, reverence, thanksgiving, and even surrender. The psalmists portray praise as an act that acknowledges human frailty even as it exalts divine perfection, reminding readers that authentic adoration involves embracing the full spectrum of human experience with honesty and humility. The vivid imagery of mountains trembling, skies rejoicing, and hearts lifting in songs of gladness beckons readers to see their own lives mirrored in the cosmic celebration of the Almighty. In this shared rhythm, the act of praising God unfolds as both a personal and communal breath, a whisper that rises to heaven and echoes through eternity.

In reflecting on these psalmic portrayals, it becomes evident that praising God serves not only as an acknowledgment of divine sovereignty but as a transformative practice—one that lifts the soul above despair, nurtures gratitude within the heart, and opens channels for grace to flow freely. The poetry of praise invites believers to recognize that in raising their voices or quiet thoughts toward heaven, they participate in a timeless chorus that connects the faithful across generations. It is in this sacred dialogue that praise transcends mere utterance and becomes a living, breathing testament to the enduring relationship between Creator and creation, a whisper to heaven that resonates with eternal life.

Living a Life of Praise

To live a life of praise is to embrace a rhythm of spirit that continuously turns the heart and mind toward the presence of the Divine, cultivating a consciousness that is attuned to the goodness, majesty, and faithfulness of God. This way of being invites believers to move beyond mere moments of worship confined to specific times or places and instead dwell in the perpetual awareness of God's glory permeating every aspect of existence. Praise becomes not only a verbal or musically expressed act but a profound posture of the soul, an ongoing dialogue that colors the mundane and the extraordinary alike with hues of reverence and gratitude. When woven into the fabric of daily living, praise transforms ordinary experiences into sacred encounters, encouraging a focus on divine grace and fostering a resilient hope even amid life's tumultuous waves.

The biblical portrait of praise breathes with urgency and tenderness alike. From the jubilant shouts of the psalmists who summon the heavens and the earth to sing along (Psalm 148), to the quiet, steady invocation of God's steadfast love in the midst of sorrow, praise is depicted as a multifaceted expression of relationship—an acknowledgment of God's unchanging nature and an invitation to participate in the divine story. Yet, living out such praise is far from a simple endeavor; it calls for intentionality and spiritual discipline to cultivate a heart that habitually recognizes and celebrates God's presence. The Psalms provide an incredible resource in this regard, illustrating how praise arises not only from triumph but also from trial, flowing both in moments of exuberance and deep lament, unified by a tender trust in God's faithful character. The longing of the psalmist's soul, articulated through poetry and song, echoes an invitation to believers today: to make praise a matter of the heart that perseveres regardless of circumstance.

Inserting praise into the tapestry of everyday life begins with an awareness that God is active and present in all things, from the dawn's first light to the sunset's rich colors, from the laughter of children to the quiet moments of solitude. This awareness births a grateful heart that ceases to take God's blessings for granted. It challenges the mind to sift through the noise of distraction and anxiety, peeling back layers of worry to find the still, small voice of divine goodness whispering in the soul. Praise, therefore, is not a reaction reserved only for when life is smooth or joyful; it is a declaration of God's nature and love, proclaimed even in the face of suffering, uncertainty, or doubt. By choosing to direct thoughts and words toward God's attributes—the holiness, mercy, power, and peace that define the Almighty—believers cultivate a spiritual lens that reframes experience, imbuing their daily walk with purpose and joy. This conscious turning toward praise shapes the interior landscape, softening a hardened heart and opening it wider to receive grace.

The spiritual significance of integrating praise into daily life is monumental. Praise acts as a bridge between the human and the divine, drawing the believer out of isolation and into communion with God. This communion is neither passive nor fleeting; it is an active, ongoing engagement that forms the foundation of spiritual growth and resilience. As the psalmist sings, "Let everything that has breath praise the Lord" (Psalm 150:6), the call extends beyond the sanctuary walls, bidding the faithful to carry the melody of worship into workplaces, homes, highways, and quiet corners of personal reflection. This constant weaving of praise is a practice of tuning one's soul to the frequency of divine love and hope, which grounds the believer in a trust that transcends the transient seasons of life. Through praise, the believer stands firm amidst chaos, uplifted by a recognition that God's sovereignty and goodness are ever constant, even when circumstances shift.

In the narrative of Scripture, praise is often the language of encountering God. Moses, after witnessing the miraculous deliverance of the Israelites, lifted his voice in unbridled song (Exodus 15), a spontaneous eruption of awe and gratitude that transformed collective memory into a shared testimony of God's power and faithfulness. Similarly, Hannah's tender prayers of thanksgiving for the gift of a long-awaited child (1 Samuel 2) reveal the heart of praise as intimately entwined with personal experience—praise as a response to mercy and answered longing. Jesus himself modeled a life infused with praise, frequently withdrawing to pray and giving thanks even before performing miracles, embodying submission and joy in the Father's presence. These biblical moments teach that praise is both a response to God's historic acts and a present-tense declaration of faith.

For contemporary readers, living a life of praise can sometimes feel elusive within the demands and distractions of modern life. The cacophony of deadlines, digital noise, and at times the burdens of despair can obscure the gentle invitation to lift one's voice to heaven. Yet, the sacred whisper that calls us into praise remains alive and vibrant beneath the surface of daily chaos. To nurture a continual spirit of praise, it is helpful to intentionally carve out moments throughout the day, to pause and reflect, to recount God's blessings, and to meditate on particular Psalms or prayers that kindle a heart of gratitude. Whether it is greeting the dawn with a whispered acknowledgment of creation's beauty, blessing the hands that prepare a meal, or silently praising the God who walks alongside in trials, these acts stitch praise into the rhythm of a lived-out faith.

Embracing praise as a lifestyle also means embracing emotional honesty in prayer, affirming that praise does not dismiss the reality of pain or struggle but holds it simultaneously within the tapestry of faith. The Psalms vividly exemplify this tension; they are filled with cries of anguish alongside soaring acclamations of God's greatness. This complexity models a prayer life that permits vulnerability without abdication of praise, a dance of confiding fears and offering adoration in tandem. Such authentic prayer nurtures a spirit untethered from circumstances, anchored instead in the character of a God who is worthy of praise not because life is perfect, but because of who God is—unchanging, compassionate, and just.

When praise permeates everyday life and prayer, it leads to transformation. A heart steeped in praise is more susceptible to spiritual breakthrough and healing. It softens bitterness, saps the strength of anxiety, and breathes hope into the weariness of the spirit. This transformation is subtle but powerful, often unfolding over time as the believer grows in recognizing the multifaceted ways God manifests grace. With each act of praise, the atmosphere shifts; relationships deepen, perspective broadens, and a spirit once weighed down by fear finds wings to soar toward peace. Praise becomes a wellspring from which courage, resilience, and joy flow, even when external circumstances remain unchanged.

Living a life of praise also impacts the community. Just as biblical psalms were often sung corporately, providing a shared language of worship and unity, praise has the capacity to connect individuals across divides. In modern contexts, communal praise can uplift churches, groups, and families, creating spaces where the sacred is acknowledged collectively, and mutual faith is strengthened. Yet, this communal praise is enriched when rooted in individual orthodox practice; each believer's personal rhythm of praise contributes to the larger chorus of faith, linking whispers of adoration from all corners of the earth in a sacred symphony. This communal dimension testifies to the fact that praise is not merely an inward experience but a relational reality that binds the spiritual family together.

Practically speaking, integrating praise into life and prayer involves developing habits and disciplines that orient the heart toward God throughout the day. Morning devotions that include praise prepare the soul for the unfolding day and fuel resilience against discouragement. Moments of stillness and reflection amid busyness offer opportunities to recalibrate focus and reengage with gratitude. Journaling blessings or praising attributes of God nurtures awareness of grace in tangible ways. Speaking praise aloud, through song or prayer, permeates the physical and spiritual being, offering a lift to the weary spirit. Over time, these disciplines build a reservoir of praise that sustains through seasons of trial and joy alike, making the soul fertile ground for the seeds of faith to blossom.

Moreover, the invitation to live a life of praise is also an invitation to embrace spiritual mindfulness—a conscious attention to the movements of God around and within. This mindfulness awakens the believer to see divine fingerprints in daily interactions, the unfolding of creation, and the quiet offering of mercy that might otherwise go unnoticed. As attention becomes attuned to these sacred moments, praise arises spontaneously, natural as breath. This spiritual mindfulness is not escapism but a grounded response that acknowledges the complexity of life while affirming God's sovereignty and presence within it.

Ultimately, living a life of praise is to participate in a sacred dialogue that unites heaven and earth. It is a proclamation of faith that speaks to the very core of what it means to be human in relationship with the Divine. The biblical examples of praise remind believers that such a life is accessible and transformative, an invitation that resonates through generations. As readers navigate their own journey, may they find in praise not only a practice but a passion—an ever-deepening connection with God that sustains, uplifts, and adorns each moment with the light of heaven. In embracing praise as a continual posture of the heart, one answers the ancient call of the psalmist: to let everything that has breath join in a harmonious whisper rising to the throne of grace—a whisper that, when carried through daily living, becomes a joyful song of gladness resonating to eternity.

Thanksgiving: Gratitude in Communion

The Spirit of Thanksgiving

Thanksgiving possesses a power that transcends simple politeness or customary ritual; it serves as a spiritual posture, an orientation of the heart that profoundly shapes the landscape of prayer and the broader experience of faith. This deeply woven thread of gratitude emerges repeatedly throughout the biblical narrative—not merely as an occasional expression of thanks but as a dynamic force that animates the soul's communion with God. To enter into the spirit of thanksgiving in prayer is to open oneself to a profound recognition of God's presence, provision, and faithful love amidst all circumstances, whether flourishing or fraught with difficulty. It is in this recognition that thanksgiving shapes both our spiritual perspective and the very texture of our lives, offering a lens through which difficulties are refracted not only as burdens but as parts of a larger divine tapestry—in which joy, hope, and resilience are knitted tightly alongside challenge and pain.

The Psalms, a treasure trove of heartfelt communication to the divine, give voice to the rich theology of thanksgiving in the ancient faith tradition. When David, often portrayed with an intimate relationship with God, erupts in songs of gratitude, he reveals the deep wells of joy that arise from recognizing God's hand in both deliverance and daily sustenance. His prayers resound with acknowledgment that God is the ultimate source of every blessing—protection, provision, justice, and peace. Rather than taking these gifts for granted, David's thanksgiving is a deliberate act of remembrance and praise, a sacred practice that anchors him even in seasons of turmoil. His words invite us into a sacred rhythm where gratitude nurtures trust and where celebrating God's faithfulness becomes a fortress against despair. Thus, thanksgiving in prayer is far more than a polite nicety; it is an expression of faith's tenacity, a conscious choosing to dwell in the light of God's goodness despite shadows on the horizon.

Beyond the Psalms, other biblical figures similarly model thanksgiving as an essential element of spiritual life, reminding us that gratitude often emerges most authentically not in moments of unbroken blessing but in the raw vulnerability of life's trials. Hannah's prayer of thanks, for instance, springs forth after years of childlessness and heartfelt petition, illustrating that thanksgiving arises from fulfilled hope as well as from the deep places of longings heard by God. The intensity of her emotions, expressed in earnest dialogue with the divine, reveals the dynamic nature of thanksgiving—it is not a static state, but a living, breathing response to God's intervention in human frailty. Her prayer invites us to see thanksgiving as inseparable from the journey of faith itself, where the heart acknowledges God's timing and wisdom even when the waiting stretches long. This posture of grateful surrender transforms prayers into sacred dialogue, a mutual exchange in which God's faithfulness elicits our praise, and our praise, in turn, opens us more fully to God's love.

Thanksgiving shapes the way believers view their own circumstances and the broader world. When gratitude occupies the center of prayer, it cultivates a spiritual perspective that transcends mere surface appearances. Life's hardships do not vanish, but they are recontextualized within God's sovereign care, allowing the heart to find rest amid uncertainty. This transformative mindset echoes the Apostle Paul's exhortation to "give thanks in all circumstances," a challenging yet liberating invitation that connects gratitude indiscriminately to every facet of life. Paul's exhortation does not demand a forced cheerfulness or shallow optimism; rather, it calls forth a deep acknowledgment that God's grace is sufficient, that His purpose is working even in moments of pain, and that thankfulness can anchor the soul in peace when external conditions might suggest otherwise. This truth reshapes prayer from a mere list of requests or complaints into an ongoing conversation steeped in awareness of God's goodness, presence, and providence.

In gratitude, we find an antidote to the corrosive effects of bitterness, entitlement, and spiritual dryness. When thanksgiving is absent, prayer risks becoming a transactional exercise, a ledger of grievances and demands with God. Yet when the spirit of thanksgiving permeates prayer, it injects humility and reverence, shaping us into individuals who do not merely seek God's gifts but delight in God Himself. Grateful prayers foster a gracious soul that sees life as gift and vocation, inviting the believer to dwell in joy rather than fixation on lack. This reminds us that even the simplest acknowledged blessings—breath, light, relationships, moments of beauty—can become portals to profound worship when held with a heart attentive to God's generosity. Thanksgiving thus acts as a spiritual magnet, drawing us closer into intimacy with the divine, transforming prayer into a sweet fragrance that ascends not only in our spoken words but in the posture of our very lives.

The example of Jesus offers the highest model for thanksgiving in prayer, illuminating how gratitude can imbue every moment of divine-human interaction with sacred significance. In the Gospels, Jesus frequently lifts thanks to the Father, publicly acknowledging divine goodness and providence before embarking on acts of healing, teaching, and ultimately sacrifice. His thanksgiving is never perfunctory but embodies a deep communion with God's will and a clear-eyed thanksgiving for God's unfolding purposes, even amidst the looming shadow of the cross. Jesus' prayers reveal that thanksgiving is not confined to triumphant moments but is integrally connected to submission and trust. In his final meal with his disciples, for instance, he gives thanks over the bread and the cup, enshrining thanksgiving as the heart of covenantal relationship and spiritual renewal. This models for believers that in thanksgiving we join Jesus' own journey of faithful obedience, echoing a heart fully surrendered and profoundly aware of God's redemptive work through all seasons of life.

When gratitude becomes the lifeblood of prayer, it also fosters a communal spirit that connects believers across time and space. The thanksgiving prayers of ancient Israel resonate still within contemporary worship—linking individual hearts to a larger body of faith history and shared experience. In this collective expression, thanksgiving functions as a unifying melody, harmonizing diverse voices in acknowledgement of God's steadfast love. This communal dimension of thanksgiving reminds us that prayer is not solely private—though it is deeply personal—but also profoundly social and spiritual. Our grateful prayers join those of saints and seekers both past and present, weaving a continuous thread that testifies to God's unchanging presence and enduring care. This realization nurtures humility and gratitude not only for God's blessings but also for the gift of community, underscoring the interdependence intrinsic to our spiritual journeys.

Moreover, thanksgiving in prayer serves as a potent catalyst for joy, an often undervalued fruit of faith that delights both heart and spirit. Genuine gratitude nurtures joy not as fleeting happiness dependent on external factors but as an abiding confidence rooted in the divine. The Psalmists frequently associate joy with the act of giving thanks, revealing an intimate linkage between the outward expression of gratitude and inward flourishing. This joy transcends circumstance, offering vitality and hope that renew strength amid weariness. Recognizing this, believers are invited to cultivate thanksgiving as a spiritual discipline that both springs from joy and feeds it, creating a vibrant cycle of grace. When prayed authentically, thanksgiving becomes a wellspring from which strength and peace flow, enabling believers to endure hardships with a resilient and buoyant spirit.

Yet the journey into the spirit of thanksgiving is not without challenges. Human nature often gravitates toward forgetfulness, dissatisfaction, and preoccupation with unmet needs or desires. In addition, the cultural milieu—saturated as it is with materialism, entitlement, and distraction—can subtly erode awareness of God's gifts and foster a posture of complaint or entitlement. To cultivate authentic thanksgiving in prayer requires intentionality and spiritual discipline, as well as a willingness to confront our own tendencies toward ingratitude. This entails developing awareness of the myriad, often unnoticed blessings that surround us and nurturing a humble heart that refuses to take them for granted. Practices such as journaling blessings, reflecting on creation's beauty, and meditative silence can open our spiritual eyes to God's providential care. Prayer becomes a sacred laboratory of gratitude, a place where God's grace is sought not only for needs but also thanked for gifts received. These intentional acts foster spiritual formation, shifting gratitude from an occasional feeling to a habitual state of being.

Furthermore, the spirit of thanksgiving in prayer cultivates a delicate balance between acknowledgment of blessings and a truthful engagement with suffering. It does not minimize pain or deny hardship but refuses to let suffering overshadow the recognition of God's presence and provision. Many biblical prayers demonstrate this tension—lament mingles with thanksgiving, sorrow with praise, vulnerability with hope. This complexity invites believers into a mature spirituality where gratitude exists alongside honesty, where the heart cries out pain even while whispering thanks. This balanced posture models the authenticity of faith and underscores that thanksgiving is not an escape from reality but a profound engagement with it, viewed through the lens of divine love. By embracing this nuance, thanksgiving in prayer becomes a beacon in the darkness, a sacred light illuminating the path where faith, hope, and love meet.

As readers enter into the spirit of thanksgiving, they are invited to consider the personal dimensions of this truth: How does gratitude reshape their own prayers? How does it transform their daily outlook? The biblical witnesses show us that thanksgiving is not reserved for extraordinary moments but is deeply embedded in the ordinary rhythms of life—arising with the dawn, accompanying the daily bread, coloring relationships with grace. When gratitude becomes the pulse of prayer, it fosters not only deeper trust in God but also openness to life's sacredness in every moment. It awakens hearts to notice beauty where once there was indifference, to rejoice where once there was despair, and to praise where once there was silence. Thus, thanksgiving breathes life into prayer, infusing it with warmth, hope, and an abiding sense of God's nearness.

In this unfolding journey, thanksgiving proves itself essential not only to prayer but to faith itself. It reveals faith's heart as one that rests in the certainty of God's goodness and embraces the full spectrum of human experience with open arms. Through thanksgiving, believers join a sacred lineage whose lips have been adorned by grateful hymns for millennia, and whose hearts continue to find solace and strength in the simple, profound act of saying "thank you" to the Divine. This spirit invites continuous return—each prayer a whisper to heaven filled with gratitude, each breath a reminder of grace, each moment an opportunity to live in the light of thankful love. The spirit of thanksgiving stands as a beacon and balm, shaping the believer's journey, shaping the face of prayer, and ultimately, shaping the soul itself.

Biblical Examples of Thanksgiving

Among the many radiant threads woven through the tapestry of scripture, the practice of thanksgiving stands out as a beacon of spiritual vitality—a practice that not only honors God but also transforms the human heart. The Bible abounds with narratives where thanksgiving emerges as a natural, profound response to divine faithfulness, creating moments of sacred dialogue ripe with joy, reverence, and recognition of God's gracious hand. This subchapter invites us to step into these biblical vignettes, to walk alongside figures like Hannah and the Israelites, who modeled hearts overflowing with gratitude, and to contemplate how their prayers of thanksgiving deepen our understanding of this vital spiritual discipline.

Hannah's story, etched within the quiet corridors of 1 Samuel, offers one of the most poignant biblical portraits of thanksgiving as a spiritual posture formed through patient longing and heartfelt surrender. She enters the narrative burdened with the deep ache of barrenness, a condition that for a woman in her cultural and religious context was more than a physical void—it was a social and existential sorrow. Yet, her approach to God is not marked by despair devoid of hope but by a prayer suffused with earnest petition that flows into a profound act of thanksgiving even before her request is fully realized. Hannah's vow, "If you will give me a son, I will give him to the Lord all the days of his life," speaks to a covenant of trust enlivened by gratitude. When Samuel is born, the boy whose name means "heard by God," Hannah moves from petition to praise, offering a prayer that exalts God's sovereignty, providence, and justice. Her song of thanksgiving, reminiscent of the Psalms, is a lyrical embrace of divine blessing that acknowledges God's ability to bring down the proud and lift the humble, to fill the barren with joy and to crown the faithful with grace. This narrative reveals thanksgiving not as a mere polite acknowledgment but as a profound spiritual response that shapes one's entire outlook, reorienting inner turmoil into jubilant surrender.

The Israelites themselves, as a collective people, provide recurring examples of thanksgiving that bind communal identity to the faithful acts of God in their history. Their journeys are fraught with trials, from deliverance from Egypt's oppressive bondage to wandering in the wilderness, yet within these trials, thanksgiving pulses as a persistent thread of recognition. The song of Moses after crossing the Red Sea, celebrated in Exodus, is a triumphant hymn that not only thanks God for deliverance but also proclaims God's power and majesty to all who hear. This communal expression of thanks serves to reinforce faith amidst uncertainty and hardship, anchoring the people's confidence in divine salvation. Similarly, the Psalms, many of which are communal songs, overflow with prayers of gratitude that celebrate God's steadfast love and wondrous deeds. Psalms such as 100 and 107 call the faithful to enter into God's presence with thanksgiving, reminding believers that gratitude is both a sacred duty and a jubilant act that releases the soul from captive worries into jubilant praise.

What stands out profoundly in these biblical expressions is how thanksgiving is woven into the fabric of spiritual resilience and joy, particularly in the midst of hardship. For the Israelites, gratitude was neither naive nor simplistic; it was a conscious choice to recognize God's providence even when the desert winds of trial blew harshly. This spiritual posture counters the despair and cynicism that so often accompany human suffering, inviting instead an acknowledgment that God's grace pervades the narrative of human existence, even when shadows fall. It is this dynamic that sets biblical thanksgiving apart from mere social convention; it is an act of trust and vision, a recognition that the divine story is ultimately one of redemption and blessing.

Returning once again to individual experiences, the narrative of Jonah, often remembered for his resistance and anger, also subtly reveals thanksgiving's place even in the unlikely journey of grace extended beyond Israel's borders. After the repentance of Nineveh, Jonah's initial reluctance yields to a grudging acknowledgment of God's mercy. Though not presented as a conventional prayer of thanks, the progression suggests how thanksgiving emerges from the recognition of God's unexpected grace—a grace so expansive it moves even the prophet to reconsider his narrowness. This subtle narrative arc invites readers to contemplate how thanksgiving might arise even in spiritual struggle or confusion, reflecting an openness to divine movement beyond personal or communal expectations.

In another striking passage, the New Testament also illumines thanksgiving as a foundational theme, weaving it into the life and teaching of Jesus and his followers. The Gospels portray Jesus frequently giving thanks—even in moments of impending suffering or self-giving. Before feeding the five thousand, for instance, Jesus blesses and gives thanks over the loaves and fishes, modeling a spirit of gratitude that sanctifies the material and invites abundance from scarcity. His prayer in the Garden of Gethsemane, though marked by anguish, incorporates submission born of trust, an implicit thanksgiving for the Father's presence, no matter the trial ahead. Early Christian epistles frequently exhort believers to "give thanks in all circumstances," a call recognizing that thanksgiving is a spiritual discipline capable of fostering peace and joy beyond the external conditions. This New Testament emphasis firmly situates gratitude not purely as a reaction to benefit but as an enduring attitude that draws believers into continual communion with God's sustaining grace.

In the figure of Mary, mother of Jesus, we find a sublime embodiment of thanksgiving and praise in her Magnificat, a song echoing the words of Hannah and the Psalms. Mary's prayer magnifies God's faithfulness through generations, expressing gratitude that leaps beyond personal joy into the cosmic realms of divine justice—"He has brought down the mighty from their thrones and exalted those of humble estate." In Mary's song, thanksgiving burgeons into a prophetic witness, linking gratitude with social transformation and hope. It invites the reader to imagine thanksgiving not only as personal solace or spiritual habit but also as a force that aligns the heart with God's larger redemptive purposes in the world.

Reflecting on these biblical examples, it becomes clear that thanksgiving in prayer functions on multiple levels. It is, first, a recognition of God's past faithfulness—a remembering of divine acts of mercy and salvation that ground one's faith in history and experience. This act of remembrance itself becomes an act of worship, a turning toward God in acknowledgment of grace received. Secondly, thanksgiving fosters a spiritual lens, reframing present circumstances and future hopes within the great canvas of God's ongoing work. Through thanksgiving, believers are invited into a posture of humility and trust, acknowledging that even unanswered questions and unfulfilled desires remain within God's providential care. Finally, thanksgiving opens the heart to joy, a deep-seated gladness that transcends transient happiness and anchors the soul in the abiding presence of God.

Moreover, the emotional richness displayed in these biblical prayers of thanksgiving underscores its significance in spiritual formation. Gratitude surfaces as a remedy against bitterness, anxiety, and despair, challenging the believer to confront honestly their circumstances while refusing to allow hardship to eclipse hope and praise. This tension, between struggle and thanksgiving, enhances spiritual authenticity, acknowledging that gratitude need not deny suffering but rather sovereignly embraces divine presence amidst it.

In the practical rhythm of contemporary spiritual life, the biblical examples stand as both encouragement and challenge. They invite readers not merely to mimic ancient words but to cultivate a posture where gratitude breathes life into daily prayers, transforming routine petitions into dialogues saturated with thankfulness. They call for the courage to bring honest, sometimes broken gratitude before God, recognizing that even lament can find its voice within a thankful heart. The stories of Hannah offering her son in joyous tribute, the Israelites raising chants of deliverance, and Mary proclaiming hope amid uncertainty inspire believers to see thanksgiving as an ongoing spiritual practice, integral to navigating the complexities of faith in a noisy and fragmented world.

Thus, the biblical portraits of thanksgiving affirm that gratitude is not a timid whisper but a potent whisper to heaven that resonates across time, offering strength, perspective, and joy to all who embrace its sacred dance. Through such prayers, hearts align with the divine melody of grace, learning to sing with confidence in life's seasons—whether in the hallelujahs of blessing or the quiet surrender of trust in the unseen. In this way, thanksgiving becomes a transformative force, inviting each reader into the timeless chorus of faithful voices who find, through gratitude, a deeper communion with God's eternal presence.

Cultivating a Thankful Heart

To cultivate a thankful heart within the sacred dialogue of prayer is to nurture a garden where the soul may flourish in the gentle light of divine grace.

Gratitude, in its deepest essence, is more than a mere custom or fleeting emotion; it is a transformative posture that aligns the heart with the eternal rhythm of God's love and provision. In the busyness of life, where worries often cloud the spirit and burdens weigh heavily, the act of consciously embracing thanksgiving becomes a radical and nourishing choice. It is within this choice that prayer takes on a vibrancy that transcends ritual, becoming a heartfelt dialogue rich with appreciation and awe. The biblical tapestry offers numerous examples, vibrant with characters who, amidst both triumph and trial, maintained an unshakable attitude of gratitude, inviting us to emulate this spiritual discipline in our own lives.

Consider the psalmist David, a man whose life was marked as much by struggle as by divine favor. His words often burst forth with raw honesty, revealing moments of despair, yet consistently entwined with praise and thankfulness. In the depths of anguish, David's prayers do not lose sight of God's enduring faithfulness; rather, they magnify it. Such an intertwining of lament and praise illustrates that gratitude is not the denial of hardship but the acknowledgment of God's presence that sustains us through adversity. By cultivating thankfulness even in dark moments, David's prayers become a beacon of hope and resilience, teaching us that a thankful heart is not blind to reality but sovereign over the soul's response to it. From this, we learn that the practice of gratitude in prayer is an act of surrender, entrusting our fears and doubts to a God whose mercies are new every morning, as the psalmist faithfully reminds us.

The narrative of Hannah further enriches our understanding of cultivating thankfulness through prayer. His longing for a child was a source of deep sorrow, yet in her fervent plea at the temple, she demonstrated a profound inner resolve—her prayer was infused not only with petition but with a promise born of hopeful trust, which would soon blossom into thanksgiving. After God's gracious answer, Hannah's song of praise echoes through the generations, a powerful testimony to the transformative power of gratitude. Her prayer invites us to approach God with openness, vulnerability, and an expectation that gratitude grows strongest when we recognize divine faithfulness in answers both immediate and unfolding. Embracing this model encourages us to lift our voices in thanksgiving not only for blessings received but for those still whispered in hope, compelling us to trust the divine timing even when our hearts ache with waiting.

To nurture a thankful heart in our prayer life requires intentionality—a deliberate shift of focus away from what is lacking toward what has been graciously bestowed. This begins with a renewed attentiveness, a spiritual discipline wherein we scan the landscape of our daily experiences for moments, both grand and subtle, where God's hand is evident. It might be the warmth of morning light, the comfort found in human kindness, or the quiet strength to face another day. These small offerings, when collected like precious stones, form a mosaic of gratitude that brightens the soul's horizon. Cultivating this attentiveness in prayer entails a gentle unburdening of the mind's chatter and a welcoming of the stillness that allows the heart to remember and rejoice. In essence, gratitude in prayer calls us into sacred mindfulness, where each breath becomes an invitation to recognize and celebrate God's ongoing presence in the ordinary and the extraordinary.

The transformative power of this gratitude lies not only in its ability to reshape our internal landscape but also to recalibrate our theological perspective. When the heart is consistently oriented towards thanksgiving, it nurtures a spiritual lens that sees life less as a series of problems to be solved and more as an unfolding story of grace. This shift enriches the prayer experience, replacing frustration or despair with trust and hope. The apostle Paul's exhortation to "give thanks in all circumstances" (1 Thessalonians 5:18) encapsulates this profound paradox: gratitude is a posture of faith that sustains even in the midst of difficulty. It does not deny suffering but erects a spiritual framework in which suffering, too, is held within God's redemptive love. Such a grateful perspective fuels perseverance, deepens joy, and invites an intimate recognition that God's goodness is not contingent upon external circumstances but is an abiding gift woven into the fabric of existence itself.

Embracing gratitude also opens the door to joyous communion, where prayer transcends the transactional and transforms into a dance of love between the human and the divine. The psalmists repeatedly express this joy through exuberant shouts, tears, and songs, revealing that thankfulness sparks an authentic emotional engagement with God. This engagement is not confined to moments of exuberance but extends into the subtle undercurrents of daily life. To cultivate this joy requires vulnerability—a willingness to lay bare the heart's true emotions, trusting that such honesty finds a loving resonance in the divine presence. Here, the paradox of thanksgiving within lament finds renewed expression: even when the soul is heavy, the spark of gratitude can kindle a flame that warms and revitalizes. Within the sacred space of prayer, cultivating a thankful heart thus becomes a spiritual anthem, sung in the quiet and in the storm alike, echoing the eternal truth that joy is deeply, irrevocably linked to gratitude.

Practically speaking, developing a habit of gratitude in prayer invites certain spiritual exercises and reflections that can gradually rewire the mind and heart. One approach is the deliberate keeping of a prayer journal dedicated to thanksgiving. By recording daily moments of gratitude, no matter how small, one creates a tangible record of grace that can be revisited during times of doubt or discouragement. This practice helps to anchor faith in concrete experiences and nurtures a growing awareness of God's active presence. Another modality involves incorporating gratitude into the rhythm of the day's prayers—beginning and ending conversations with God through acknowledgments of thanks for the breath, the body, the relationships, and the opportunities entrusted to us. Even in brief moments of prayer, such acknowledgments can serve as spiritual touchstones that tether the heart to humility and joy.

Moreover, cultivating a thankful heart need not be confined to solitary prayer but flourishes profoundly within communal settings. The biblical tradition frequently underscores the power of collective thanksgiving, as seen in the psalms chanted by congregations and in prayers offered by groups united in faith. Participating regularly in communal acts of worship where gratitude is expressed through song, spoken prayer, or silence grounds the individual in a larger spiritual family. This shared practice often magnifies gratitude, as communion with others can deepen the emotional and spiritual resonance of thankful expressions. The mutual witnessing of God's faithfulness in community fosters a collective identity rooted in grace, encouraging each participant to carry that spirit of thanksgiving beyond the worship space into daily life.

Relational gratitude, expressed both upward toward God and outward towards others, holds a unique place in the cultivation of a thankful heart. As one recognizes the many ways God expresses love through the people around us, prayer becomes a channel through which we acknowledge and honor these divine gifts embodied in human kindness. Interweaving thanksgiving into prayers for others deepens empathy and nurtures a spirit of generosity, echoing the biblical injunction to "rejoice always, pray without ceasing, give thanks in all circumstances." This relational dynamic transforms prayer from a self-centered act into a vibrant encounter with the interconnectedness of the body of Christ. By regularly lifting up others in prayer with grateful hearts, the practitioner of prayer learns to celebrate the life-giving presence of God moving through every interaction, weaving an ever-strengthening fabric of grace.

It is also crucial to recognize that nurturing gratitude in prayer is often a gradual unfolding rather than an immediate transformation. The spiritual landscape of the heart is frequently complex and layered, where past wounds or persistent struggles may resist the simple embrace of thanksgiving. In such seasons, grace allows for the presence of honest lament alongside the slowly blossoming seeds of gratitude. The journey toward a thankful heart may involve patience, gentle perseverance, and the willingness to return again and again to the throne of grace, even when the spirit is weary. This perseverance itself is a form of thanksgiving, a silent acknowledgment of dependence on God's sustaining love. The biblical narrative offers no promise that gratitude will come easily but instead reveals a divine companionship that walks beside us through the valleys, nurturing a fragile but growing hope that blossoms into deeper thankfulness over time.

Furthermore, the cultivation of gratitude in prayer invites the believer into a renewed awareness of the nature of God's character. When we reflect on the scriptures, God emerges as a faithful lover, a provider who meets needs, a healer who restores, and a guide who never abandons. Recognizing these attributes through the lens of thanksgiving refines the spiritual focus, encouraging prayers that honor God's goodness rather than merely seeking favors. This spiritual refinement leads to a prayer life that is not merely about receiving but about participating in the ongoing recognition of divine grace that permeates creation. As gratitude deepens, prayer becomes less about asking and more about celebrating, less about anxiety, and more about awe. This shift fosters a richer experience of God's presence—a presence that invites us into a dance of love so intimate and vast that our very whispers can become echoes of heaven itself.

In this light, cultivating a thankful heart imperatively includes moments of intentional silence and reflection. In our era of constant noise and distraction, carving out sacred stillness is vital to allow gratitude to take root. Silence in prayer offers a space where the heart can listen and the spirit can breathe, where Thanksgiving arises not from the clamoring mind but from the serene depths of being. It is in these moments of quiet contemplation that the fullness of God's blessings can be apprehended, not as achievements or possessions but as gifts freely given. Establishing regular rhythms of stillness and meditation within the prayer life fosters an environment where gratitude flows naturally, no longer forced but emerging like a river unbidden, sustaining the soul through every season.

Finally, as this journey toward a thankful heart unfolds, it becomes clear that gratitude is not merely a human offering to God but a divine invitation into a deeper fellowship. Gratitude connects us across the centuries, linking our own whispers to heaven with the hymns of the ancients and the prayers of saints yet unborn. It is in this shared spiritual lineage that thanksgiving becomes a sacred legacy—one that invites each individual to contribute their voice to a chorus of praise that transcends time and space. By embracing gratitude in prayer, we join with biblical figures like David and Hannah, Mary and Solomon, creating a living testimony that honors God's faithfulness while opening our souls to the profound joy and peace that only a thankful heart can fully experience. Through this sacred cultivation, prayer transforms from obligation to celebration, from routine to revelation, and from solitude to communion, drawing us ever closer to the heart of God, where all thanks eternally converge.

Confession: Healing Through Honesty

The Purpose of Confession

Confession, in its deepest and most transformative sense, stands at the very heart of spiritual vitality and the profound dialogue between the soul and the divine. To confess is to lay bare the hidden corners of one's inner life, to reveal the fractures and failings that threaten to obscure the radiant light of God's grace. It is a sacred act of truth-telling, an acknowledgment not merely of failure but of the yearning for restoration and intimacy with the Creator. In the biblical narrative, confession emerges as an indispensable step toward spiritual health, for it ushers the believer into a space where divine mercy can flow unimpeded, where the soul may be cleansed and renewed. Without this act of honest reckoning, prayer risks becoming an exercise of pretense or self-delusion, severed from the healing balm that only God's forgiveness imparts. The purpose of confession, then, transcends the mere cataloging of wrongs; it is a deliberate embrace of vulnerability before the holiness of God, a courageous journey from the shadows of guilt into the liberating light of grace.

Throughout the Bible, confession is presented not as a burdensome requirement of religious law but as a gateway to transformation and hope. The Psalms frequently illustrate this profound dynamic—David, a man after God's own heart, does not shy from articulating his sins with piercing honesty. His voice trembles with the weight of his transgressions, yet it also courses with the vibrant trust that God's mercy is sufficient to absorb the depths of human frailty. In Psalm 51, his penitential prayer stands as a timeless example of confession's power. As David unwraps the reality of his guilt before God, he simultaneously opens himself to the possibility of renewal, pleading for a cleansed heart and a spirit steadfast within him. This act of confession is not merely a confession of facts but a heart laid bare in longing for restoration. The psalm reveals that the soul is not healed by denial or avoidance but by entering into the honest reality of sin and receiving God's grace that makes all things new.

The act of confessing sin has a remarkable psychological and spiritual function: it creates the conditions for reconciliation and freedom. When sin is acknowledged honestly, it loses its power of secrecy and shame, which often imprison the soul in isolation and despair. The confession breaks the chains that bind, admits the rupture that sin causes not only between the individual and God but within the self. This self-exposure, though difficult and sometimes painful, is an act of liberation, akin to a cleansing flood that washes away the debris clinging to the heart. Biblical figures such as King Manasseh, who after years of prideful rebellion, humbled himself in repentance, demonstrate how confession can turn the course of a life. Manasseh's admission of guilt before God, as recounted in 2 Chronicles, leads to a profound restoration that offers hope not only to him but also to all who contemplate the grace that awaits those who humbly turn to the divine presence.

Moreover, confession nurtures a dynamic transformation in the praying soul by fostering spiritual humility. In a world often dominated by pretenses of perfection and the illusion of self-sufficiency, confession bursts forth as a radical act of dependence on God's mercy. It humbles the proud heart, which clamors for control and self-justification, and invites it into the gentle embrace of divine compassion. As the prophet Isaiah conveys through God's word, the sacrifice that pleases the Lord is a broken spirit; a contrite heart is more precious than any outward religious ritual. Thus, confession reveals itself as a cleansing river for the soul, a channel through which God's purifying presence flows most deeply. It restores relationship—not through human merit, but through the grace that welcomes the penitent, who acknowledges not only the reality of sin but the greater reality of God's faithful love.

Confession also connects deeply to the communal aspect of faith and spiritual growth. Though it is a private dialogue between the individual and God, its implications often flow outward into relationships and community life. Sin rarely affects only the individual; its ripples extend to family, community, and even the wider creation. By confessing sins, believers break the cycle of secrecy and unspoken burdens that can poison relationships and disrupt communal harmony. The prophetic tradition in the Bible frequently calls Israel to confession not merely as private contrition but as public acknowledgment of collective failure—sins that hurt the community and stifle the witness to God's kingdom. This model reminds believers today that confession is never solitary in its impact; it is a path toward healing and restoration that benefits both the individual and the body of Christ. When believers confess, they open a breach in the walls of isolation, building bridges toward reconciliation and renewed fellowship.

In the New Testament, confession takes on fresh dimensions through the teachings of Jesus and the apostles, further underscoring its indispensable role in spiritual vitality. Jesus, through his ministry, affirms the necessity of repentance and confession, calling people not only to seek forgiveness but to embody a spirit of humility and transformation. The story of the sinful woman who anoints Jesus's feet with tears—her confessions washing him with fragrant balm—illustrates the depth of intimacy and healing that confession enables. The apostle John explicitly teaches that "if we confess our sins, he is faithful and just to forgive us our sins and to cleanse us from all unrighteousness," reinforcing confession as the conduit through which divine forgiveness and purification flow. John's words echo the enduring truth that confession is not an end in itself but a means by which the soul is restored to wholeness and communion with God.

Moreover, confession has a liberating power that extends even beyond the immediate experience of forgiveness. It invites the believer into an ongoing process of spiritual renewal, a persistent turning back to God that deepens over time. This iterative nature of confession means the soul is continually detoxified from the corrosive effects of sin, gradually shaped into the likeness of Christ. The daily practice of confession, whether articulated aloud, silently meditated upon, or written in the quiet solitude of one's heart, keeps the believer tethered to divine grace. It resists the complacency and spiritual blindness that so easily creep in when one assumes sin is absent or minimal. Confession sharpens spiritual awareness, heightens sensitivity to God's presence, and opens the door for healing beyond the immediate moment. This continuous rhythm fosters resilience and hope, empowering believers to navigate the complexities of a fallen world with a steadfast trust in God's tender mercy.

In practical terms, confession also revitalizes prayer by stripping away the barriers that sin erects between the soul and the divine. Sin often accrues layers of deflection, excuse, and concealment, which act like a veil that dims the clarity of spiritual vision and dulls the intimacy of communion. When the soul refuses or neglects to confess, prayers can become mechanical, empty rituals that fail to touch the heart's deepest longings or engage with God's transformative power. The act of confession strips these layers away, revealing the raw and unvarnished truth of the self before God. This vulnerability invites a response not of condemnation but of grace, strengthening the believer's trust that prayer is a sacred dialogue where one need not hide or pretend. As confession clears this way, prayer regains its dynamic and exploratory vitality, opening new horizons of spiritual growth and relational depth.

The theology of confession is inseparable from the biblical understanding of God's nature as both just and merciful. God's justice entails holiness that cannot countenance sin; simultaneously, divine mercy sweeps beyond human failure to restore and heal. This tension is revealed beautifully in the biblical drama of confession, where the sinner encounters both divine judgment and mercy. Far from contradicting one another, these aspects converge in the act of confession, which becomes the moment where fallen humanity meets resurrecting grace. This meeting is a sacred paradox: in admitting faults, the believer is not condemned but embraced, not discarded but renewed. It is this divine dance between justice and mercy that makes confession powerful beyond measure, turning a seemingly simple act of word into a transformative encounter with the living God.

In essence, confessing sins nurtures an ever-deepening relationship with God, one rooted in honesty and the mutual desire for wholeness. It acts as a spiritual mirror reflecting not only the brokenness but also the infinite capacity for renewal inherent in all who seek God's face. The purpose of confession is thus far more than a remedial act following moral failure—it is a sacred pathway that invites believers into ever-closer communion, an ongoing reception of divine light that penetrates even the darkest corners of the soul. By embracing confession, the believer aligns with a biblical tradition that honors transparency as the foundation for intimacy with God, where the whispers of the heart rise unburdened to heaven and receive in return the gentle caress of grace.

As the modern believer stands at the intersection of ancient scriptural example and contemporary spiritual practice, understanding confession's profound purpose can transform the way prayer is lived and experienced. It challenges the tendency toward self-sufficiency and denial, inviting instead a posture of openness and dependence. Confession thus becomes a sacred rhythm interwoven with all other forms of prayer, a vital ingredient for maintaining spiritual health and vitality. It teaches that spiritual growth is not a straight path of flawless progress but a journey that embraces imperfection, brave vulnerability, and the continual seeking of divine mercy. In this sacred dialogue, the soul finds rest, healing, and the courage to rise anew—whispers to heaven that echo with the eternal promise of forgiveness and transformation.

Confessional Prayers in the Bible

In the vast landscape of biblical prayer, confessional prayers hold a profound and sacred place, revealing the soul's vulnerable encounter with divine mercy—an unguarded, heartfelt admission of human frailty that becomes a gateway to renewal and hope. Nowhere is this more poignantly illustrated than in the penitential psalms attributed to King David, a towering yet deeply human figure whose prayers walk us through the intimate terrain of confession with a raw honesty that continues to resonate across millennia. David's prayers are not mere ritualistic recitations of guilt, but vibrant, soul-stirring dialogues that lay bare the complex nuances of remorse, repentance, and the yearning for divine restoration. They invite us into the sacred space where acknowledgment of sin transforms into an embrace of grace, illustrating that confession is not an endpoint but a vital beginning of spiritual rebirth.

To enter the world of David's confessional prayers is to witness a man grappling with the full weight of his moral failings—not in defiance, but in a posture of deep humility. Consider Psalm 51, often hailed as the quintessential lament of confession, composed in the shadow of a grave personal crisis. Here, David's soul cries out amidst the wreckage of his transgressions, beseeching God for mercy with an intensity that burns through the pages of scripture. "Have mercy on me, O God, according to your steadfast love; according to your abundant mercy blot out my transgressions," he implores (Psalm 51:1). Within this single opening line flows the essence of confession: a recognition of wrongdoing paired with the urgent appeal for forgiveness rooted in God's unwavering compassion. David does not attempt to veil his faults or excuse his actions; rather, he exposes them fully, demonstrating the courage required to approach God with honesty and contrition.

The emotional texture of David's confession is richly layered, capturing the turmoil that comes with the awareness of sin. There is sorrow, yes, but also a profound sense of desperation and longing for inner renewal—a desire not merely to be forgiven but to be fundamentally transformed. "Create in me a clean heart, O God, and renew a right spirit within me" (Psalm 51:10). This plea reveals confession's deeper spiritual purpose: to clear away the debris of guilt and shame, opening the heart to receive divine grace that sparks a new beginning. Confession, in this light, is an act of healing, a sacramental moment where brokenness meets balm, and where the spiritual vision of a cleansed and restored self begins to take shape. David's prayer reverberates as a timeless testimony that confession is not a passive admission of guilt but an active turning toward God's renewing power.

The theological richness of these confessional prayers also underscores the indispensable role of repentance as a form of spiritual discipline. David's prayers emphasize the necessity of inward transformation—not just ritualistic or external acts designed to appease God, but profound change in the heart and mind. He acknowledges, "For I know my transgressions, and my sin is ever before me" (Psalm 51:3), highlighting a consistent and conscious awareness that sin is more than a momentary lapse; it is a condition that must be confronted and overcome through ongoing repentance. This awareness leads to a contrite and humble spirit, which Psalm 51 beautifully describes as "a broken and contrite heart, O God, you will not despise" (Psalm 51:17). Here, the biblical narrative dispels any notion that confession is a mere formality; it is a transformative encounter where divine forgiveness is extended not to those who presume on mercy lightly, but to those who approach with genuine remorse and resolve to change.

David's confessional prayers are not isolated instances in scripture but resonate with the broader biblical witness that confession is an essential element of the believer's journey toward God. From the ancient covenant traditions that insist upon acknowledging sin before worship to the New Testament's insistence on confession for reconciliation and healing, the act of admitting faults is intertwined with the experience of grace. For instance, the prophet Daniel's prayer in chapter nine echoes this confession motif, in which he openly admits the collective sins and the rebellious state of his people. Daniel's prayer is communal as well as personal, underscoring how confession functions not only at the individual level but also within the corporate life of faith communities, inviting fellowship in vulnerability and forgiveness.

The spiritual dynamics woven through these prayers also highlight the paradox that confession—though often accompanied by feelings of shame or fear—actually liberates the soul from the bondage of hidden sin. David's willingness to bring his transgressions into the light exemplifies the biblical truth that secrecy breeds isolation, but confession invites restoration and reconciliation. This dynamic is intensely relevant for modern readers, reminding us that the discipline of confession in prayer is not simply about unburdening guilt, but about opening ourselves up to God's sanctifying work. The vulnerability of exposing our faults before the divine altar beckons us beyond self-justification and denial into an empathetic awareness of our need for God's redemptive love.

Beyond David, other biblical figures also model the power and efficacy of confessional prayers, demonstrating the multifaceted role confession plays throughout scripture's narrative. Consider the story of the prodigal son, whose return to the father involves a confession not so much of specific sins but of a humble heart acknowledging failure and seeking restoration. This parable highlights confession as an act intertwined with repentance and the experience of being embraced anew. Similarly, the public confession of King Manasseh, a ruler notorious for his sins, marks a turning point not only in his personal destiny but in the life of the nation. His prayer of confession and repentance leads to divine forgiveness, illustrating God's readiness to restore even those who have deeply erred.

In reflecting on the nature of these confessional prayers, it is vital to appreciate how they invite us into a prayerful posture of honesty, where the act of naming our shortcomings becomes an intimate spiritual encounter. Confession draws us into a sacred rhythm of breaking and mending, exposing and healing. It enables us to confront the shadowed corners of our hearts with courage and trust, knowing that God's response is not condemnation but compassion. In this way, confessional prayer serves as a powerful spiritual tool, fostering a deeper awareness of our human limitations while simultaneously drawing us closer to the boundless mercy of God.

The theological implications extend further as confessional prayers challenge us to embrace an ongoing journey of sanctification. David does not simply confess and move on; he seeks purification and a steadfast spirit, reflecting the transformative potential embedded in confession. This ongoing process opens the way for spiritual maturation, where the believer becomes increasingly attuned to God's presence and guidance. The confessional prayer thus becomes a mirror reflecting our need for continual renewal, a call to live not in denial but in a transparent relationship with the divine.

Practically, the example of David's penitential prayers offers timeless guidance for cultivating a confessional practice in contemporary spiritual life.

They teach us that confession requires a safe, reverent space where vulnerability is honored and where prayer leads to healing, not guilt-induced paralysis. Learning from David's example encourages us to approach confession with faith in God's mercy, embracing honesty as a strength rather than a weakness. The confessional prayers model the emotional breadth necessary for genuine contrition—from anguish and remorse to hope and surrender—reminding us that spiritual renewal demands the whole heart's engagement.

Moreover, these prayers reveal how confession intersects with the broader tapestry of prayer, seamlessly integrating with praise, thanksgiving, and supplication. David's prayers, for example, often conclude with expressions of praise and trust despite the gravity of confessed sin, reflecting a dynamic interplay where confession becomes the soil from which deeper gratitude and faith emerge. This spiritual movement underscores that confession, far from being a gloomy admission, is an act of hope grounded in the trustworthiness of God's covenant love.

In essence, the confessional prayers found in the biblical narrative, and epitomized through the poignant voice of David, illuminate the sacred dialogue of sin and forgiveness—a delicate yet powerful exchange that invites us to lay down our burdens and be lifted by grace. These prayers testify to the enduring truth that our imperfections need not separate us from the divine embrace; rather, in sincere confession, we find the path to spiritual restoration and the whisper of heaven's abiding mercy. To engage with these prayers is to embark on a transformative pilgrimage, one that beckons us to confess not only our sins but also our deepest longing for God's healing touch, nurturing a faith that is authentically humble, deeply penetrating, and vibrantly alive.

Practicing Confession Today

In the quiet sanctuaries of our minds and hearts, the practice of confession unfolds as a sacred dance—a revealing of the soul's inner landscape before the compassionate gaze of the Divine. To confess is to step into a vulnerable space, where honesty meets humility, and human frailty is laid bare not to shame but to healing. It is within this space that spiritual renewal breathes, casting light upon the shadows of our conscience and inviting grace to mend what is broken. Although ancient in its biblical roots, confession remains undeniably vital in the rhythm of contemporary prayer life, offering a profound pathway toward reconciliation with God, oneself, and community. Practicing confession today is more than an act of ritualized admission; it is a courageous embrace of truth that paradoxically frees us into wholeness and peace.

When we look back at the biblical tapestry, we see figures like King

David, who epitomizes the raw vulnerability of confession in Psalm 51. His prayer is not merely a recounting of sin but a poignant outpouring of remorse, an aching plea for mercy that paints the profound emotional contours of contrition. David's willingness to acknowledge his transgressions before God invites readers into a similarly honest encounter, encouraging an authenticity that defies superficiality. In our modern practice, confession can emulate this sacred transparency, encouraging us to name our shortcomings with specificity and sincerity. To do so, one must carve out moments within the busyness of life, moments of intentional stillness where distractions are silenced, and the heart's murmurs can be heard in their unvarnished truth. This might mean beginning with a quiet meditation, allowing thoughts to settle like sediment, or perhaps journaling reflections that unpack the tangled threads of regret, envy, anger, or selfishness that bind us.

One of the beautiful paradoxes of confession is that although it stems from recognizing our faults, it opens the door to a deeper experience of God's grace rather than closing the door through guilt or condemnation. The biblical narrative ceaselessly resounds with this theme; God's response to confession is not judgment but mercy, igniting transformation and restoration. Practicing confession today entails cultivating a trust in that divine kindness, an assurance that by naming our brokenness, we are met not with rejection but renewed acceptance. This trust is not always easy to muster, especially in a world that often equates mistakes with failure or unworthiness. Yet prayerful confession reminds us that the heart of spirituality beats in vulnerability and that the Divine longs to heal, uplift, and draw us back into wholeness. When we participate in confession with this expectation, the practice becomes a profound form of spiritual medicine—anointment for the wounded soul.

Practically speaking, incorporating confession into one's personal prayer routine invites creativity and openness. There is no prescriptive formula or rigid liturgical pattern that must be followed exactly; rather, confession is an intimate dialogue tailored to the individual's needs and spiritual temperament. Some find that articulating their confessions aloud, either in solitude or within the safe communal embrace of a trusted spiritual mentor or congregation, deepens the sense of accountability and connection. Others might prefer the silent offering of confessions in prayer, a tacit conversation felt rather than spoken, carried in the depths of the heart. The use of written confession, through prayer journals or letters addressed to God, has proven transformative for many, allowing one to articulate weaknesses and regrets with clarity, charting a spiritual journey of openness and renewal over time.

A powerful practice to enhance confession today is to ground it in scripture, inviting the Word of God to shape and illuminate the confession itself. The Psalms, in particular, offer a rich reservoir of prayers that express contrition and seek mercy. Praying a Psalm of confession before articulating one's own sins connects the individual to a timeless community of faith, echoing ancient voices that confessed and found liberation. Additionally, reflecting on Jesus' teachings about forgiveness, such as the parables of the prodigal son or the unmerciful servant, offers poignant reminders of God's willingness to forgive and the transformative power of grace. Integrating these scriptural passages into prayer practice can help reframe confession from a purely self-focused exercise to a participatory act in the ongoing story of divine redemption.

Moreover, practicing confession today encourages us to consider the relational dimension it fosters—not only between the believer and God but also within the community. While personal confession nurtures individual renewal, confessing to another person, when feasible, reflects the biblical call toward communal accountability and healing. James 5:16 exhorts believers to "confess your sins to one another and pray for one another, that you may be healed." This dimension invites vulnerability within safe spaces marked by trust and love and can be profoundly liberating. In contemporary contexts, this might manifest in spiritual direction, therapy with a faith component, or support groups where honest sharing is honored, and healing is sought collectively. Confession, then, becomes a conduit of grace beyond the private realm, knitting hearts together in mutual support and encouragement.

The emotional landscape of confession today is richly complex, demanding sensitivity and courage. It requires sitting with uncomfortable feelings—shame, regret, sorrow, and sometimes a deep sense of unworthiness—without allowing these feelings to define one's identity. The image of confession as a gentle uncovering rather than a harsh self-judgment can shift internal dynamics, helping individuals approach this spiritual discipline with compassion rather than dread. Cultivating a habit of self-forgiveness alongside confession is crucial, ensuring that one's acknowledgment of missteps leads toward restoration rather than despair. This emotional honesty can also be a catalyst for profound personal growth, as it pushes the faithful to confront patterns that hinder spiritual flourishing, opening the door to transformation through God's sustaining grace.

In contemporary life marked by noise, haste, and often superficial interactions, carving intentional time for confession is itself an act of rebellion—a reclaiming of spiritual depth and authenticity. It can begin with small but deliberate steps: setting aside a few moments daily to examine one's conscience, inviting the Spirit to illuminate areas needing healing, and gently offering these to God with honest words. This rhythm creates a sacred cadence that nurtures a keen awareness of God's presence and grace throughout the day. Spiritual disciplines such as fasting or retreats can also intensify the practice of confession, providing an immersive setting that invites deeper self-examination and renewal. Ultimately, these varied approaches honor the multifaceted ways in which God meets different souls, calling each to an authentic and personal encounter with divine mercy.

Confession practiced today does not exist in isolation but is often intertwined with other forms of prayer, enriching the entire spiritual tapestry. For example, after confessing faults and seeking forgiveness, many find themselves moved into prayers of thanksgiving for God's redemptive mercy. Confession can also lead naturally into intercessory prayer, as having faced one's own brokenness fosters greater empathy and compassion for the struggles of others. This interconnectedness shows prayer not as segmented or compartmentalized but as a dynamic flow within one's spiritual experience, where confession is a vital step that opens the heart for deeper communication with God and others. It reminds believers that spiritual renewal is a holistic journey, marked not only by admission of sin but also by an ongoing commitment to growth, grace, and love.

The technology and cultural shifts of the modern world present both challenges and opportunities for practicing confession today. On one hand, the distractions and relentless pace of digital life can draw attention away from reflective spiritual practices, making it harder to find quiet moments for honest self-assessment. On the other hand, technology also offers tools for nurturing confession: apps dedicated to daily reflection, virtual spiritual communities, and online confession forums provide new avenues for engagement. While these cannot replace deeply personal and embodied encounters with God and trusted spiritual companions, they offer supplementary spaces where believers can practice honesty and receive encouragement. The key lies in thoughtful discernment, ensuring that these tools serve to deepen rather than dilute the sacredness of confession.

Infused with humility, confession practiced today becomes a profound gateway to experiencing God's unfailing love and transformative grace. As the Bible reveals, the courage to admit faults does not weaken the believer but strengthens the soul's capacity to receive healing and renewal. It aligns the human heart with divine will, opening avenues not only to forgiveness but also to a life reshaped in integrity and faithfulness. For the modern seeker, embracing confession in personal prayer routines is a way of echoing the timeless whispers to heaven—an invitation to draw near to God with an open heart, ready to be restored.

Through this practice, the ancient rhythm of contrition and grace continues, knitting the faithful across generations in a sacred dialogue that brings light into the shadows and invites the soul into the fullness of divine peace.

Lament: Expressing Sorrow and Seeking Comfort

The Nature of Lament

Lament, as a form of prayer, penetrates the depths of human experience with a rawness and vulnerability that transcends everyday speech. It is not merely a cry of sorrow or complaint but a sacred encounter where the soul's anguish is brought into the direct presence of God. The nature of lament invites us to confront the realities of pain, loss, confusion, and injustice without retreat or disguise, offering a space where honest emotions can be expressed with spiritual candor. In the biblical landscape, lament emerges not as an aberration but as a profound and legitimate posture before the Divine, one that acknowledges the fractured condition of the world and the human heart while seeking restoration, justice, and comfort. Its significance is multi-dimensional, bridging the psychological, emotional, and spiritual realms and underscoring the holistic nature of prayer as a dialogue that encompasses every facet of our existence.

At its core, lament is the embodiment of grief articulated through faith's language. It acknowledges the deep rupture caused by suffering—whether that be the loss of loved ones, betrayal, persecution, personal failure, or the overwhelming presence of evil and despair—while refusing to sever the connection with God. In lamentation, the heartache is neither minimized nor masked; rather, it is laid bare before the sacred, inviting God's attentive presence into the void left by pain. The Psalms, often called the prayer book of the Bible, provide the richest treasury of lament, revealing a pattern of wrestling through despair toward a renewed trust in God's faithfulness. For instance, Psalm 13 opens with a desperate question, "How long, Lord? Will you forget me forever? How long will you hide your face from me?" yet concludes with a confident declaration of hope, "But I trust in your unfailing love; my heart rejoices in your salvation." This movement—from raw lament to tentative hope—illustrates the transformative power inherent in this type of prayer, allowing the psalmist to process grief within the embrace of divine grace rather than in isolation.

The significance of lament extends beyond its function as emotional expression; it serves as a form of spiritual catharsis, a purgative dialogue that can heal the interior wounds inflicted by suffering. Human beings are created for relationship, and pain threatens to isolate us from others and, crucially, from God. Lament reclaims that relational dimension by verbalizing anguish in God's presence, thereby refusing silence or anonymity in the face of distress. This act of vocalizing grief codifies suffering as worthy of divine attention and honors the sacredness of human pain. Rather than suppressing the uncomfortable or inconvenient reality of sorrow, lament echoes the honesty of biblical figures who, in their brokenness, dared to approach God without pretense. Hannah's pleading for a child in 1 Samuel 1 is suffused with such lament: her silent lips move while her heart is "deeply troubled," and she pours out her soul before the Lord, not holding back tears or anger. Her lament becomes a conduit of hope, transforming anguish into petition and opening her life to the possibility of God's intervention.

Moreover, lament sustains a theological tension—the tension between suffering and hope—that lies at the heart of biblical faith. In embracing lament, believers affirm that pain and hardship are real and impactful, yet they resist despair by anchoring their cries in the character of a faithful and compassionate God. This tension enables lament not only to express grief but also to challenge God's apparent silence or absence. It asks the difficult questions: "Why has this happened? Where is your justice? Do you see my pain?" Such queries, far from undermining faith, represent its most honest and engaged dimensions. Lament holds God accountable, seeking answers without forfeiting trust. It embodies covenantal intimacy, wherein the believer risks exposing the deepest hurts in hopes of divine response. This intricacy evokes a spiritual dialogue that does not simplify suffering but enriches faith by insisting on its presence within the framework of relationship with God.

The form of lament prayer is often marked by its poetic and emotive qualities, utilizing metaphor, repetition, and direct address to convey the speaker's burden. The psalms provide numerous examples of this artistry, illustrating how lament combines expressive language with theological reflection. The invocation of God's name amid tears, the recounting of past faithfulness, and the declaration of trust amid doubt enrich the texture of lament and invite the reader or pray-er to enter into the emotional ebb and flow with empathy and understanding. The communal aspect of lament is also significant; many laments publicly voice the pain of a people or nation, such as the communal laments following exile found in the Book of Lamentations. These prayers attest to the importance of shared sorrow, demonstrating that lament is not merely a personal expression but a collective act that knits communities together in their search for meaning and consolation under the shadow of suffering.

The psychological and emotional dimensions of lament cannot be underestimated. Modern theological psychology recognizes lament as a vital process for emotional health, allowing individuals to confront trauma, anger, fear, and disappointment rather than repress them. The act of lamenting openly before God provides a safe container for these emotions, facilitating healing through acknowledgment and spiritual companionship. This process nurtures resilience, helping believers to withstand despair and find renewed strength in the knowledge that they are not alone in their pain. It also dismantles the false notion that faith requires stoic silence in the face of suffering, instead portraying a spirituality that welcomes honesty and emotional depth.

From a pastoral perspective, lament models an essential component of spiritual maturity: the courage to bring one's brokenness into the light of God's presence. It counters the cultural stigma around grief and vulnerability by affirming that lament is a holy act, a form of worship that honors God through its authenticity. This shapes a theology of prayer that values candor over piety, depth over superficiality. Pastoral ministry benefits from this understanding by providing individuals with permission to lament freely, recognizing that through lament, God meets us in our lowest moments and sustains us with grace and hope. It thus becomes a crucial resource for healing congregations and individuals traversing seasons of loss or crisis.

Another profound aspect of lament's nature is its hopeful dimension. While lament begins in suffering, it frequently concludes with an expectant turn toward God's deliverance or mercy. This pivot contains a theological assertion that God is not indifferent to human pain and that restoration is possible. The very structure of biblical laments suggests a journey from complaint to comfort, from despair to trust, inviting believers to hold space for pain while embracing the promise of God's redemptive presence. It enshrines hope as a vital counterbalance, assuring the believer that sorrow is not the final word and that in aligning their cries with God's compassionate heart, they participate in the mystery of healing and renewal.

In contemporary spiritual practice, embracing lament challenges modern sensibilities that often prioritize positivity, productivity, and denial of suffering. Lament, by contrast, teaches the invaluable lesson that faith grows deeper when it incorporates grief and questions alongside praise and thanksgiving. It fosters a prayer life that is robust and honest, a sacred conversation that refuses to bypass pain but rather invites God's compassionate presence into the storm. By recognizing lament's nature as an essential, sacred form of prayer, readers are encouraged to reclaim their own voices amid hardship, trusting that their honest whispers to heaven meet a God who hears, understands, and transforms.

Ultimately, the nature of lament in prayer is a testament to the breadth of human experience embraced within the life of faith. It affirms that the journey toward God includes moments of darkness and doubt, that prayer is not always a serene landscape but often a rugged path marked by tears and questions. Lament invites believers to move beyond superficial comfort toward a deeply relational encounter with the Divine, where suffering is neither ignored nor eliminated but held within the mysterious space of God's love. In this sacred dialogue, lament becomes not only an expression of sorrow but a powerful conduit of hope, sustaining the soul with a resilient trust that no shadow is beyond God's light, and no cry is lost amidst the heavens. Through lament, prayer embraces the full spectrum of human vulnerability, affirming that to whisper to heaven is to speak the truth of the heart with courage, honesty, and faith.

Examples of Lament in Scripture

Within the sacred scrolls of Scripture, the voices of those who have lamented rise with a raw, poignant power that transcends time and envelops the reader in the profound depths of human sorrow and divine engagement. These voices, found vividly within the Psalms and echoed through the prophetic books, invite us into the sacred space where anguish becomes a bridge to communion with God. Lament is not mere complaint; it is a dynamic, deeply vulnerable conversation that cracks open the heart to reveal the complex dance between pain and hope, despair and trust. To engage with these biblical examples is to witness the multifaceted nature of lament, a form of prayer that embraces honesty before God without losing sight of His ultimate sovereignty and compassion.

The Psalms stand as the richest tapestry of lament in the biblical canon, offering a profound window into the psyche of those wrestling with affliction. For centuries, they resonated as the spiritual anthem of a people intimately acquainted with suffering, exile, loss, and oppression.

Psalms such as Psalm 22, which begins with the haunting words, "My God, my God, why have you forsaken me?" encapsulate the visceral experience of feeling abandoned by God, a sentiment echoed in the anguished cries of Jesus on the cross. This psalm unravels the layers of despair with a transparency that is both unsettling and deeply human, yet it resolutely turns toward hope, concluding with an affirmation of God's deliverance and future praise. Here, lament is not a static wallowing but a pilgrimage from the shadow of death into the light of divine faithfulness.

Similarly, Psalm 42 unfolds as a poetic journey of yearning when the psalmist declares, "As the deer pants for the water brooks, so pants my soul for You, O God." The imagery is exquisite, revealing an emptiness and a thirst so profound that they threaten to consume the speaker. The psalm articulates a restless sorrow and a heart weighed down by unrelenting circumstances, yet it refuses to surrender entirely to despair. Within these verses lies an embodiment of the spiritual tension at the core of all lament: the groaning of a soul in distress, coupled with a persistent cry, "Hope in God; for I shall yet praise Him," refusing to let go of trust even when all seems lost. This oscillation between grief and hope is characteristic of biblical lament and serves as an enduring model for anyone seeking to pray through pain.

The Psalms are also remarkable for their communal laments, where the voice of individual sorrow melds into a collective outcry. Psalm 44, for example, portrays the weary lament of a nation that feels betrayed by God's apparent silence amidst adversity. The psalmist recounts past divine intervention, highlighting a contrast between earlier deliverance and present suffering. This communal lament exposes the complexity of faith when faced with inexplicable suffering, where trust in God's promises wrestles with the stark reality of hardship. The plaintive questions, "Why do You hide Your face? Why do You forget our affliction?" echo across generations, validating the raw questions and doubts that believers may bring to God when endurance wanes. Yet, even these cries resound with a refusal to sever the relationship with the Divine, as the psalmist clings to the covenantal bond, embodying a lament that is both deeply broken and firmly anchored.

Beyond the Psalter, the prophetic writings further enrich the biblical landscape of lament by integrating personal sorrow within the broader context of covenantal judgment and hope. The prophet Jeremiah, often called the weeping prophet, embodies lament not only as prayer but as a prophetic lamentation cascading over a nation in turmoil. His heartfelt cries are etched with sorrow for the destruction of Jerusalem, the exile of his people, and the perceived silence of God. In Jeremiah 20, the prophet voices his anguish with raw brutality, describing how he has become a man of strife and contention, cursed by those who hear his lament. Yet, amidst the despair, Jeremiah's prayers reveal a gripping honesty that refuses to mask pain or feign faithfulness. They lay bare the paradox of serving God amid rejection and suffering, allowing readers to witness lament as both a burden and an act of faithful courage.

The Book of Lamentations, traditionally attributed to Jeremiah, stands as a solemn hymn of communal lament over the fall of Jerusalem. Its poetic verses cascade like tears over the ruins, painting vivid pictures of devastation, starvation, and profound loss. The language is enveloped in a mournful cadence, giving voice to a people shattered by catastrophe. Yet woven through this tapestry of grief is a resilient thread of hope: "The steadfast love of the Lord never ceases; His mercies never come to an end; they are new every morning." This poignant refrain encapsulates the didactic purpose of lament—it is not only a confession of sorrow but an invitation to lean into divine mercy amidst desolation. Through these passages, the reader encounters a lament that is simultaneously honest to the depths of despair and transparent with trust in God's unyielding compassion.

The prophets Hosea and Habakkuk likewise weave lament into their cries against injustice and cultural decay. Hosea's prayer-lament, suffused with personal and national betrayal, portrays the anguish of a broken covenant relationship, which he describes with intimate pathos. His words reveal a heart torn by unfaithfulness, yet accompanied by a desire for restoration. Habakkuk, on the other hand, wrestles intensely with the problem of divine justice, questioning why God permits wickedness to flourish while the innocent suffer. His laments echo the existential questions often raised in dark seasons of faith, providing a pattern for wresting with doubt without abandoning devotion. The prophet's eventual resolution—to "quietly wait for the salvation of the Lord"—offers a luminous path through the thickets of confusion and despair that characterize lament.

The laments within Scripture also include an intensely personal dimension in the prayers of individual biblical figures, notably Hannah, Job, and David. Hannah's silent, fervent prayer in the temple, captured in 1 Samuel, is a poignant example of the intimate lament of a barren woman anguished over her childlessness. Her prayer is heavy with sorrow but esteemed by God, ultimately leading to the gift of a son. This narrative reveals lament's transformative power—how the act of bringing pain before God can open the door to renewal and blessing. Job's story, perhaps the archetype of lament, is a theological and existential odyssey of pain and questioning. His unflinching honesty before God—his cries of confusion, protest, and yearning—challenge any simplistic notion of suffering. Job's lament underscores the complexity of faith amid inexplicable loss and the paradoxical intimacy between questioning and worship that genuine prayer embodies.

David, a man after God's own heart, provides a multifaceted portrait of lament throughout his life. His psalms frequently move between despair and declaration of faith, embodying the candid emotionality evident in human sorrow and divine reliance. Whether fleeing Saul's persecution or grappling with personal sin, David's prayers reflect the acute depth of human vulnerability pouring out before God's throne. His laments are not only expressions of distress but teach us how to balance complaint with praise, acknowledging suffering while leaning into God's sustaining mercy. David's example affirms that lament is not weakness but a robust spiritual discipline enabling believers to bring the entirety of their experience to God's presence.

The theological richness of lament in Scripture emerges from the tension between vulnerability and hope—a dialectic at the heart of faithful prayer. The biblical laments teach that prayer is not a monologue of thanksgiving but an honest and dynamic dialogue that holds sorrow, confusion, anger, and yearning alongside praise and trust. This interplay invites readers to embrace the fullness of their spiritual selves, affirming that God honors the honesty of brokenness and responds with grace. Lament serves as a spiritual sanctuary where grief is neither suppressed nor left to fester but is nurtured into a voice that transforms suffering into hope.

In modern spiritual practice, these biblical laments stand as powerful models for navigating personal and communal grief. They encourage believers to engage with God authentically, not shying away from the stark realities of pain but entering into a sacred dialogue that brings both catharsis and renewal. The ancient laments remind us that within the depths of sorrow flows the possibility of encounter with the Divine, that our cries are heard and held, and that even amid chaos and silence, God's steadfast love remains—a whisper breathed into the tumult, beckoning the soul toward light and life.

As readers immerse themselves in the psalms of lament and the prophetic prayers of sorrow, they are invited into a sacred companionship with those ancient voices. This communion transcends chronology and culture, proving that lament is an enduring form of prayer—at once deeply human and profoundly divine, a channel through which the faithful heart pours out its anguish while grasping the promise of God's unwavering presence. Through these scriptural examples, believers find both permission and encouragement to bring their own laments before God, trusting that their whispers are heard in the heavens and that in the sacred dialogue of lament, transformation, and healing quietly unfold.

Healing Power of Lament

Within the sacred tapestry of biblical prayer, the profound expression of lament holds a unique and healing place, inviting the human soul to lay bare its suffering, confusion, and sorrow before the unyielding presence of the divine. Lament, often misunderstood or shunned in contemporary spiritual conversations for its raw vulnerability and sorrowful tone, emerges in the Scriptures not merely as an outpouring of grief but as a transformative journey marked by honesty, trust, and ultimately, renewal. To explore the healing power of lament is to recognize prayer as a dynamic encounter where brokenness is not hidden but revealed and redeemed within the comforting embrace of God's steadfast love. The ancient voices who lamented in the biblical text, from the anguished cries of David to the tearful pleas of Hannah, invite every seeker into a sacred space where honesty with God becomes the soil from which new life springs.

Lamentation begins in the shadow of pain, grief, and loss, reflecting the genuine human experience of suffering. The Psalms provide a vast reservoir of lament prayers, where sorrow is expressed with unflinching directness. Psalm 13, a profound example, captures the deep loneliness and desperation of one who feels forgotten and abandoned, crying out, "How long, O Lord? Will you forget me forever?" This unvarnished expression of hurt reveals the biblical comfort in not masking our pain but voicing it fully before God. Such lament does not weaken faith; instead, it testifies to a relationship so intimate that no emotion, even despair, is withheld. This unburdening itself carries a therapeutic essence, allowing the afflicted heart to release the choking tightness of grief. In these moment of lament, prayer ceases to be ritualistic or performative and becomes a real, vulnerable conversation where the individual acknowledges their frailty and the depth of their need for divine intervention and solace.

The cathartic function of lament is evident in how it acknowledges the reality of anguish without denying the presence of God. The biblical lament embraces a paradoxical posture: it confronts pain head-on while holding fast to the hope that God listens and acts. Jeremiah's lamentations, filled with overwhelming distress for the destruction of Jerusalem, show a prophet wrestling fiercely with God's silence and judgement, yet never abandoning his ultimate faith in God's covenantal promise. Such prayers carve a sacred space where sufferings are mourned yet held in the tension of trust. This dynamic tension is essential to the healing journey, illustrating that lament is not despair's endpoint but a gateway to spiritual renewal. By honestly naming the gap between present pain and promised hope, lament cultivates both awareness of human limitation and reliance upon divine mercy. In this regard, lament is akin to a furnace in which despair is refined into hope, resignation into expectant waiting.

This transformative process of lament is deeply intertwined with spiritual comfort. The biblical texts teach that to lament is to participate in an ancient tradition of faith that acknowledges God as a refuge in times of trouble. When the Psalmist cries out, "The Lord is near to the brokenhearted," the healing power of lament is clarified: it is through giving voice to brokenness that the soul experimentally discovers the nearness and tenderness of God. The act of lamenting draws the believer closer to God, not by bypassing suffering but by bringing it to God's feet, acknowledging that true comfort arises not from escaping pain but from meeting God within it. This encounter fosters a spiritual intimacy that renews the weary heart and transforms sorrow into a wellspring of resilience. In this way, lament stands as a sacred dialogue that validates suffering yet refuses to let it dominate the existential narrative, replacing isolation with divine companionship.

Moreover, lament often carries a hopeful dimension that transcends the immediate distress. The lamenting prayers of biblical figures ultimately find voice in trust and praise, suggesting that lament is never intended to be an end in itself but a passage toward healing and restoration. This progression can be witnessed in the Psalms, where after confessing heart-rending grief, the Psalmist frequently turns toward expressions of faith and hope, affirming God's steadfast love and salvation. For those engaged in personal lament, this movement toward hope offers a spiritual framework where lament becomes a means to reclaim the power of trust amid turmoil. The process encourages believers to embrace their grief without succumbing to despair, nurturing a spiritual resilience that carries them through the darkest nights. Thus, lament functions as a bridge from sorrow to renewal, inviting a deepening of faith and an enlivening of spiritual courage.

Practically speaking, engaging with lament in prayer challenges modern believers to confront the cultural discomfort around expressions of suffering and vulnerability. In a world that often prizes stoicism, control, and positive thinking, lament calls forth a countercultural posture of openness that honors pain rather than suppressing it. The biblical lament reminds us that God is not threatened by our tears or questions but welcomes the honest transparency of a heart laid bare. This truth can be profoundly liberating, providing a spiritual permission slip for those who carry hidden burdens, to unburden themselves to God. Through lament, prayer becomes a sanctuary for the soul's healing, a place untouched by judgment where raw emotions can be safely expressed and held. The acknowledgment of suffering in prayer leads to an emotional catharsis that nurtures healing and prepares the soul to receive divine grace anew.

Beyond individual healing, lament embodies a corporate dimension, offering a voice to communal grief and injustice. The biblical narratives recognize that suffering is often shared and that lament can serve as a communal cry for mercy and restoration. The collective laments of the Israelites in exile, lamentations over the destruction of the temple, and prophetic laments over societal sin vividly demonstrate how lament functions as a spiritual response to communal trauma. These joint expressions of sorrow forge collective resilience, fostering solidarity among the afflicted and turning shared pain into collective hope. In this way, lament transcends personal healing and becomes a catalyst for communal renewal, inviting communities to bring their brokenness before God collectively, trusting in divine restoration.

Importantly, the healing power of lament also unfolds within the broader context of God's redemptive narrative. Biblical lament does not turn away from the reality of evil, injustice, or suffering; it names these evils frankly and petitions for divine intervention, illustrating a profound engagement with the problem of suffering that is often rendered invisible in sanitized spiritual approaches. Yet this unflinching confrontation with the harshness of life is suffused with a quiet confidence that God's justice and mercy will ultimately prevail. The trust inherent in lament anticipates the fidelity of God's promises, the restoration of righteousness, and the consolation of the afflicted. This eschatological hope—the conviction that pain is temporary and will give way to divine redemption—serves as a wellspring of courage and endurance for those who lament. Thus, lament is inherently hopeful and redemptive, opening a spiritual space where suffering is neither ignored nor allowed to dominate, but integrated into a larger story of salvation.

The biblical witness also reveals how lament is intricately connected with other forms of prayer and spiritual expression. It intertwines with confession, repentance, and intercession, highlighting the holistic nature of spiritual healing through prayer. When the Psalmist laments the pain caused by sin or calls on God to intervene on behalf of others, lament becomes a multidimensional experience of spiritual cleansing, advocacy, and renewal. This rich interweaving of prayer forms underscores that lament is far from a passive expression of sorrow; instead, it is an active, engaged dialogue that seeks transformation for oneself and others. The integration of lament into the rhythm of prayer life nurtures a balanced spirituality that embraces the fullness of human experience, celebrating joy and hope as well as mourning and struggle.

Finally, the healing power of lament finds expression in its invitation to cultivate a posture of humility and surrender before God. To lament is to admit human limitations and fragility, to recognize that life's sufferings sometimes overwhelm our capacity to understand or control. This vulnerability is not a weakness but a doorway to grace, inviting God's intervention and comfort in profound ways. The spiritual surrender embedded in lament becomes a release of control, a letting go that opens the heart to divine healing and renewal. This humble acknowledgment of human need draws the believer into a deeper reliance on God's sustaining presence, a foundation upon which faith is tested, refined, and ultimately strengthened. Within this surrender lies the paradox of lament: though born in sorrow and weakness, it becomes a source of strength, resilience, and hope.

In sum, the healing power of lament manifests in its authentic acknowledgment of suffering, its cathartic release, and its hopeful progression toward renewal and restoration. The biblical prayers of lament provide a sacred map for spiritual healing, guiding the soul through the labyrinth of pain toward the light of God's presence and comfort. By embracing lament as a vital form of prayer, the believer is invited to transform grief into grace, despair into hope, and isolation into divine fellowship. This ancient dialogue between the human heart and the divine invites all who suffer to approach God not with masks or silence but with honest and vulnerable whispers to heaven, confident that in this sacred exchange lies the balm for a wounded spirit and the promise of new spiritual life.

Intercession: Praying for Others

What is Intercession?

Intercession, a profound expression of prayer that reaches beyond personal needs and petitions, stands as a sacred bridge between the divine and the collective human experience. It is a spiritual act that invites the believer to step into the role of advocate and mediator, lifting the burdens, hopes, and hearts of others before God's throne. At its essence, intercessory prayer is an offering of oneself on behalf of another, a selfless lifting up of needs that resonates with both compassion and divine purpose. This form of prayer extends beyond mere words; it is an intentional and powerful embrace of another's life, a spiritual commitment to stand in the gap, to plead, to beseech, and to petition the Almighty for mercy, guidance, healing, and blessing not for oneself, but for one's neighbor, community, nation, or even the wider world. Intercession embodies the sacred mystery by which the human spirit, touched by love and concern, becomes a vessel of divine grace, a conduit through which heavenly intervention and transformation may flow.

When we examine the biblical roots of intercession, we enter a landscape rich with characters whose prayers became the very lifeblood of their people's survival and flourishing. Among the towering figures who give us vivid examples of intercession, Moses stands unparalleled as both the quintessential intercessor and the embodiment of a heart wholly devoted to God and his people. Throughout the Exodus narrative, Moses repeatedly intercedes on behalf of the Israelites, standing before God in moments of divine judgment and mercy, pleading for their deliverance and forgiveness. This is not a mere ritualistic act but a profound spiritual encounter reflecting breathtaking intimacy with the divine will. When the

Israelites rebel and provoke God's righteous anger, it is Moses who lays his soul bare before God, imploring him not to destroy the children of Israel. His intercession reveals a powerful theology—prayer as a means of partnership with God in the unfolding of redemption, as a loving, courageous act of supplication born from intimacy and responsibility. Moses' words serve not only as petitions but as a passionate declaration of God's covenant faithfulness, reminding both heaven and earth of the promises that hold through generations. The striking image of Moses standing in the breach, taking upon himself the consequences of his people's sin and pleading for their rescue, exemplifies the profound burden and blessing of intercessory prayer.

Equally significant is the New Testament portrayal of Jesus as the ultimate intercessor, whose prayer life reveals the heart of divine intercession in its fullest and most perfect form. In Hebrews 7:25, we are told that Jesus "always lives to make intercession" for those who come to God through him, casting him not only as our Redeemer but as our eternal Advocate. Jesus' intercessory prayers underscore a profound spiritual reality: that intercession is a divine ministry, an eternal act of love and mediation between a holy God and fallen humanity. His prayer in the Garden of Gethsemane, where he pleads for the cup of suffering to pass from him yet submits wholly to the Father's will, reveals the paradox of intercession—that it embodies both personal surrender and vicarious petition. Jesus prays not only for himself but with and for human beings caught in the turmoil of sin, fear, and separation from God. His intercession is a model of the delicate balance between divine sovereignty and human responsibility, between submission and advocacy, reflecting the depths of divine empathy and the heights of sacrificial love.

The biblical narrative also draws attention to the communal and relational aspect of intercession, suggesting that it is not merely a private spiritual discipline but a dynamic act that shapes communities and alters destinies. Characters like Abraham intercede for the cities of Sodom and Gomorrah, negotiating with God over the fate of the righteous within the city. This episode reveals intercession's function as a prophetic dialogue, in which prayer engages not only hearts but also justice. Abraham's audacious bargaining with God echoes the tension between justice and mercy, highlighting the intercessor's role as one who pleads for grace amidst judgment, who dares to trust in God's compassion while confronting divine holiness. This exchange unveils the power of intercession to influence divine decisions and to embody the hope that mercy can triumph without compromising truth.

In understanding intercession through these biblical portraits, it is essential to recognize its profound spiritual dynamics—intercession is at once an act of love, courage, faith, and hope. It demands of the intercessor a unique vulnerability, a willingness to open one's heart to the pain and needs of others, to stand in solidarity with their suffering and struggles. Yet it also requires deep faith in God's power and promises, the steadfast conviction that prayer is not a passive or futile exercise but an active posture of trust that can bring about real transformation. Intercession is woven into the fabric of divine-human interaction, a sacred rhythm where human cries meet divine ears in a dance of mercy that reshapes lives and situations.

Moreover, intercession bears a profound responsibility, a sacred charge to pray with intentionality and humility, mindful that the intercessor's voice echoes in the chambers of eternal love. This responsibility calls for a prayerfulness that is disciplined, persistent, and informed by scripture and spiritual wisdom, preventing intercession from becoming simply wishful thinking or mechanical repetition. Instead, it blooms into a vibrant ministry of partnership with God, a spiritual warfare against forces that oppose healing, peace, and redemption. The intercessor becomes a spiritual warrior, wielding prayer as a weapon and a shield, standing against injustice, sickness, despair, and dark powers, embodying God's resolve to restore and bless creation.

Additionally, biblical intercession highlights the element of relationality; it is deeply communal, reflecting the interconnectedness of human lives and destinies under God's governance. It teaches that no one is truly isolated in their spiritual journey; rather, believers are called to hold one another up in prayer, reflecting the body of Christ, where each member cares for the others. This communal prayer cultivates empathy, nourishes spiritual bonds, and fosters collective healing and renewal. Intercession thereby becomes both a gift and a discipline rooted in love, compelling believers to carry each other's burdens and to pray not only when convenient but as a faithful expression of their covenantal relationship with God and neighbor.

Examining the broader biblical landscape, we see how intercession is not limited to extraordinary figures or singular moments but is invited of every believer called into God's kingdom. The Scriptures encourage the faithful to engage in intercessory prayer with boldness and love, modeling after the examples of Moses, Jesus, and the prophets. This democratization of intercession opens a sacred space where every whisper, every heartfelt plea lifted on behalf of others, weaves into a great chorus reaching heaven's ear.

Such prayer transcends time and culture, bridging the gap between the needs of a hurting world and the unchanging heart of God.

In reflecting on this sacred calling, one realizes that intercession is at once a deeply spiritual and profoundly human response to the suffering, challenges, and aspirations that surround us. It embodies a willingness to enter the shadowed places of human experience with hope and faith, to carry the light of God's presence into those darkened spaces through prayer. This understanding reframes prayer from a solitary activity to an act of participation in divine redemption, aligning the intercessor's heart with God's eternal purposes. Through intercession, the believer embraces the high calling to participate in God's work of restoration, healing, and blessing on Earth, becoming a channel of grace and mercy flowing from heaven to those in need.

Thus, intercession, grounded deeply in scriptural truth and exemplified by biblical intercessors, emerges as an indispensable dimension of a vibrant prayer life. It reveals the transformative power of prayer not only to affect circumstances but to change hearts—including the heart of the intercessor—and to draw individuals into a fuller experience of God's compassion and justice. It challenges the believer to move beyond self-centered prayer and to embody the heart of God, whose love extends beyond all borders and embraces all who suffer or hope. In answering this call, intercessory prayer becomes a living testimony to the enduring reality that prayer is not merely about speaking to God but about standing in God's presence as advocates for one another, united across time and space in a sacred dialogue that truly whispers to heaven.

Biblical Intercessors

Throughout the sweeping narrative of Scripture, the profound role of intercession emerges as a sacred bridge—where the voice of one stands in the gap for many, lifting burdens and petitions before the Almighty. Within this grand tapestry, certain figures stand illuminated by their exceptional dedication to praying for others, embodying the potent, sometimes perilous, calling of the intercessor. It is not merely a peripheral role but one of extraordinary intimacy with both God and humanity, a spiritual vocation that demands courage, compassion, and an unshakable conviction in the power of prayer. The stories of these biblical intercessors reveal not only their personal faith journeys but also the larger divine drama in which their prayers intertwined with the fate of whole communities and, indeed, the unfolding of salvation history.

Among the most seminal figures in this lineage is Moses, the quintessential intercessor whose relationship with God and Israel paints an intimate portrait of mediation. From the very outset of Israel's exodus from Egypt, Moses strides forward as the voice calling out for liberation and protection, his prayers echoing across the wilderness toward a responsive heaven. Moses' intercession begins when the burdens of the enslaved people overwhelm him and yields to an audacious dialogue with God—so candid and human that it reveals the heart of intercession as both a plea and a profound partnership with the divine will. Notably, when the people rebel, complaining about their hardships and even worshipping a golden calf in blatant defiance, Moses does not recoil or abandon them but instead presses God's mercy with unyielding fervor. His prayers are not polite requests but passionate urgings that reflect both justice and compassion, a delicate balance between pleading for forgiveness and standing firm for righteousness. Moses, through his intercession, reveals the heavy responsibility carried by those who pray for others, as his heart vulnerably opens to their failings and to God's righteous judgment.

The narrative tension in Moses' intercessory role is deeply instructive: he is both the voice of the people and the servant of God's justice, embodying the paradoxical stance every intercessor must assume. He often enters the divine presence, standing "between the living and the dead," embodying the biblical mandate that prayer is more than personal consolation—it is a profound act that carries consequences for entire nations. Moses' perseverance, especially during the pivotal moments when Israel's fate seemed precarious, underscores the power inherent in intercession as an act of spiritual warfare, where words become weapons shaped by faith and persistence. His unwavering commitment at Sinai and throughout the Wilderness journey, when the people's murmurs threatened to dissipate God's promised blessings, cements his legacy as the archetypal intercessor whose prayers shaped history and positioned Israel to receive God's covenantal promises.

Yet, the role of intercessor does not end with Moses; it finds its fullest expression in the person of Jesus, whose entire ministry embodies the intercessory love of God incarnate. The Gospels and the Epistles reveal Jesus not only as the ultimate mediator between God and humanity but also as the supreme intercessor, who at once prays for others and invites his followers into a shared participation in this sacred vocation. Jesus' prayers, often described as moments of intimate communion with the Father amidst his public ministry, model the posture of intercession—marked by empathetic petition, surrender to divine will, and relentless grace. His prayer in the Garden of Gethsemane unmasks the emotional and spiritual weight borne by those who intercede. In his sorrow and anguish, Jesus wrestles with the prospect of suffering, yet ultimately submits with the words, "Not my will, but yours be done." This surrender crystallizes the heart of intercessory prayer: it is not a demand but a willing offering, a sacred dance between personal anguish and divine intention.

Furthermore, Jesus' high priestly prayer recorded in John 17 culminates his intercessory ministry as he petitions for his disciples and those who will believe through their word. Here, the themes of unity, protection, and sanctification converge, revealing intercession as a bridge not only between individuals and God but also among the community of believers. His prayers embody the tender, all-encompassing care of God extending through human agency, a model for all who would bear the mantle of intercession. Jesus teaches that intercession is not an isolated endeavor but a communal act of spiritual solidarity, drawing followers into the heart of God's redemptive mission. His example thus sacralizes the role of the intercessor as both advocate and friend of God, whose whispers to heaven carry the weight of love and cosmic hope.

Beyond these towering figures, the Scriptures bring to life other compelling examples of intercessors whose prayers moved mountains and shaped destinies. Abraham, called "the friend of God," frequently interceded when divine judgment hovered over Sodom and Gomorrah. His bold negotiation with God, asking to spare the cities if ten righteous people could be found, reveals intercession as an act of fearless advocacy grounded not in self-interest but in the welfare of others. Abraham's dialogue with God reflects a profound confidence in God's mercy and justice, highlighting intercession as an intimate conversation marked by respect, urgency, and faith in divine compassion. Though

Sodom's fate was ultimately sealed, Abraham's words illustrate the tension and hope that characterize intercessory prayer—a willingness to stand before God's holiness with honesty and boldness.

Similarly, the prophet Samuel stands in the annals of intercession as a figure whose prayers bridge national destiny and personal devotion. As Israel's spiritual leader during turbulent times, Samuel interceded repeatedly for the people, especially at moments when their rebellion threatened to sever their covenant with God. His prayerful mediation between God and the people is emblematic of the intercessor as a spiritual shepherd, who not only brings petitions but also embodies repentance and supplication on behalf of a wayward flock. Samuel's role underscores the transformative potential of intercession, where prayer becomes a catalyst for renewed covenantal relationship and divine blessing. His life encapsulates the burdens and blessings of intercession, revealing it as a ministry of hope amid judgment.

The poignant prayers of Hannah, the mother of Samuel, also illuminate the path of intercession through a deeply personal lens. Her earnest supplication for a child in the midst of barrenness culminates in a vow of dedication, illustrating how intercession reaches beyond mere requests to a sacred covenant of trust and surrender. Hannah's prayer, filled with raw emotion and honest lament, exemplifies intercession as both invocation and trust, where the intercessor offers not only their words but their whole being into God's hands. Her story affirms that intercession includes the intimate, heartfelt cries that shape faith and deliverance in deeply personal ways.

In the prophetic books, figures like Jeremiah and Daniel emerge as intercessors whose prayers embody both lament and hope, pleading for mercy amidst impending judgment. Jeremiah's laments over Jerusalem reflect a heart intertwined with the fate of his people, his prayers revealing the sorrow and persistence of an interceding heart burdened for a nation facing exile. Daniel, on the other hand, offers fervent supplications that include confession on behalf of his people's sins, exemplifying intercession as a holy encounter where personal devotion carries communal responsibility. Their prayers cast intercession as a sustained act of faithfulness during times of crisis, in which the intercessor holds firm to hope and divine promise amid overwhelming odds.

These biblical portraits broaden our understanding of the intercessor's role beyond privilege or position, unveiling intercession as a ministry grounded in empathy, courage, and the willingness to bear others' burdens. The intercessor's prayer becomes a sacred act of solidarity, rooted in a deep awareness of human frailty and divine mercy. In these stories, prayer transcends ritual to become an active, earnest engagement in the divine-human narrative—a sacred dialogue that transforms both the supplicant and those for whom they plead.

Moreover, the experiences of biblical intercessors reveal that their prayers often require wrestling—sometimes with God's apparent silence, other times with the tension between justice and mercy. Their stories teach that intercession is not a passive activity but one fraught with spiritual struggle, an arena where faith is forged and refined. The intercessor must hold space for divine mystery while passionately advocating for grace, embodying a trust that God hears even when answers are delayed or differ from expectation. This perseverance through uncertainty highlights intercession as a pathway to spiritual maturation, where the intercessor learns to discern God's will and align their heart with divine purposes.

These narratives also illuminate a vital theological truth: that intercession is a ministry invested with responsibility and authority, yet one that requires humility and dependence on God. The intercessor, by standing between God and humanity, participates in a divine plan that transcends personal gain, embodying servant leadership and covenantal faithfulness. Moses, Jesus, Abraham, Hannah, Samuel, Jeremiah, Daniel, and other intercessors remind us that prayer is an act of deep connection—linking human vulnerability with divine power, communal need with transcendent grace.

For modern readers, these powerful biblical examples serve as both inspiration and challenge. They invite us to reconsider prayer beyond self-focused desires and to embrace the possibility of standing in the gap for others through intercession. The spiritual posture of the intercessor calls us to be attentive to the burdens of those around us, to cultivate empathy expansive enough to carry the needs of others into the presence of God. Intercession, as modeled by biblical figures, requires an open heart willing to enter the pain and joys of community, an unwavering faith that our prayers can indeed influence heavenly action and earthly transformation.

In our contemporary spiritual landscape, often marked by individualism and distraction, learning from these biblical intercessors offers a profound counter-narrative—a call back to the sacred art of standing in the gap. Through their stories, we glimpse the power of prayer to act as a conduit of healing, justice, and divine blessing, urging believers to approach prayer as a communal and transformative practice. The intercessor's ministry thrives not only in grand moments of crisis but also in the quiet, persistent lifting of voices, the whispered prayers that embody steadfast love and hope.

Ultimately, the biblical intercessors teach us that to pray on behalf of others is to enter into a sacred covenant of love, courage, and faith—one that transcends time and circumstance. They invite us into a prayer life marked by compassion and perseverance, by honest dialogue with God and bold advocacy for the needs of others. Standing in their footsteps, we too can nurture our whispers to heaven, knowing that intercessory prayer is a vibrant and vital expression of our spiritual journey, capable of moving hearts and shaping destinies just as surely today as it did in the ancient days. In the interplay of lament, petition, surrender, and praise, the intercessor's voice becomes a powerful melody in the eternal symphony of divine-human communion.

Practical Intercession

Intercessory prayer, the sacred act of standing in the breach, lifting the burdens and hopes of others before the throne of God, is both a profound privilege and a compelling responsibility. It is the holy space where the heart extends beyond its own confines, reaching into the tangled complexities of human need and divine possibility. The biblical image of intercession unearths a truth deeply woven into the fabric of spiritual life: prayer is never truly solitary. From the anguished pleadings of Moses, who begged the Lord to spare a rebellious people, to the tender and powerful prayers of Jesus, who interceded with unyielding love for the very ones who would betray and abandon Him, we glimpse the transformative rhythm of communion that transcends self-interest. This form of prayer invites us, as readers and believers, to participate in the eternal dialogue of grace, where hearts align with God's will not only for ourselves but also for our communities, nations, and the world.

To cultivate a habit of intercessory prayer is to embark on a journey that begins in the quiet chambers of the soul and flows outward into the world's needs with both urgency and compassion. It calls for a deliberate opening of spiritual eyes and ears, a readiness to listen deeply to the voices of others that might otherwise be muffled by the noise of daily life. At first, this practice may seem daunting—how does one bear the weight of so many troubles without being overwhelmed? Yet, biblical intercessors teach us that we are not alone in this task. Moses, for all his human frailty, modeled vulnerability alongside courage; his prayers were raw, evocative, sometimes confrontational, but always rooted in a steadfast hope in God's mercy. His example encourages those who feel unworthy or uncertain to approach intercession with honesty, trusting that God's grace meets us not in our perfection but in our willingness to carry one another in prayer. Similarly, Jesus' intercessory prayer in the Garden of Gethsemane, pleading not for His own relief but for the protection and sanctification of His disciples, offers a compelling blueprint for selfless, loving intercession. His prayers encompass divine surrender and compassionate advocacy, aspects of the practice that nurture both the intercessor and the one prayed for.

In embracing the habit of intercessory prayer, the first step is cultivating intentionality—prayer no longer happens by chance or only in moments of personal crisis but becomes a disciplined devotion, part of daily rhythm. This conscious commitment invites the intercessor to keep a 'prayer ledger' of sorts, a mental or written record of names, situations, and struggles that ignite their spiritual empathy. Anchoring these intentions with scriptural promises fosters perseverance when the urgency fades or answers seem delayed. The Psalms, rich in lament and praise alike, offer language and emotional texture to support prayers that lift others from despair to hope. For instance, Psalm 121, with its assurance of God's unfailing guardianship, can strengthen a prayer warrior's heart in lifting the vulnerable, affirming that even when human efforts falter, divine protection endures.

But intercession is not merely a matter of mind or ritual; it demands deep engagement of the heart and spirit. Developing this form of prayer habit means allowing empathy to soften boundaries and expand perceptions of interconnectedness. It is in these moments of sacred encounter that the intercessor begins to experience a subtle transformation, feeling God's heartbeat for the world and the specific lives interwoven with their petitions. This shared spiritual burden kindles a profound resilience and hope that sustains the practice. Scripture reveals recurring instances not only of God hearing such prayers but of prayer itself shaping the course of human and cosmic events. The narrative of Abraham's pleading for Sodom, the persistent widow who would not cease asking for justice, and Daniel's fervent appeals on behalf of his people, affirm the potent role of intercession as sacred advocacy over the temporal realm. These stories invite modern believers to trust that no earnest prayer is wasted—that divine attentiveness is ever active, oriented toward restoration and mercy.

In practical terms, building habits of intercessory prayer benefits from rhythms that enable sustained focus and heartfelt expression. Beginning each day by lifting specific names or situations to God, perhaps in moments of quiet before the rush begins, roots the practice in gratitude and hope. Setting alarms or reminders can help weave intercession into the day's fabric, preventing it from being sidelined by distraction. Prayer journaling, too, opens a vital space to pour out emotions, track answered prayers, and discern evolving needs. Such records become sacred artifacts of faithfulness, encouraging perseverance through dry seasons when the echoes of supplication seem distant. Incorporating petitions into communal worship and small group settings deepens mutual support and accountability, reflecting the biblical principle that prayer is both personal and corporate. Sharing intercessory lists fosters a dynamic where burdens are not borne in isolation but embraced in the fellowship of believers.

While these practices enhance discipline, the heart of practical intercession remains relational and incarnational. The discipline gains depth and vitality when intertwined with acts of kindness, advocacy, and presence. Prayer calls the intercessor to more than words; it beckons toward embodying compassion as a tangible response to the needs prayed over. Jesus' model of intercession is inseparable from His ministry of healing and justice, revealing that authentic prayer flow moves both upward toward God and outward into the world. Intercession nurtures an intimate awareness of God's heart for the marginalized, the suffering, and the hopeful. This awareness compels the prayerful to become instruments of peace and healing—a bridge between heavenly petition and earthly action. In this way, intercession remains vital and relevant, grounded in the lived realities of others' joys and sorrows.

Moreover, the role of the Holy Spirit in guiding and empowering intercession cannot be overstated. As believers grow in prayerful attentiveness, they learn to discern the Spirit's nudgings—when to pray fervently, when to remain silent in trust, when to intercede with joyful expectation, and when to persist through spiritual resistance. Romans 8 speaks profoundly of the Spirit interceding with groanings too deep for words, reminding the intercessor that even in moments of silence, prayer continues, carried by divine presence beyond human articulation. Recognizing this spiritual dynamic emboldens prayer warriors to step beyond their limitations, trusting that God's power works through their frailty and finite understanding. It offers a sacred partnership where human initiative and divine sovereignty coalesce in the ongoing dance of sacred intercession.

It is also essential to address the challenges inherent in cultivating a sustained practice of intercessory prayer. The weight of others' suffering can induce weariness or even spiritual discouragement. There are times when prayers seem unanswered or when the pain witnessed through prayer does not diminish, stirring doubts and frustration. Yet, the biblical witnesses remind intercessors that perseverance is a hallmark of faith and that prayer itself is transformative for the one who offers it. The psalmist's laments, Daniel's fasting and prayer, and Jesus' tearful prayers depict a landscape where lament and hope coexist, underscoring that divine dialogue embraces complexity rather than denying struggle. Encouraging intercessors to embrace their own vulnerability as part of the spiritual process fosters a sustainable and authentic practice, one that honors the fullness of human emotion as it pours out before God.

In cultivating practical habits, intercession also invites the prayerful to remember the eternal perspective, that their prayers resonate beyond immediate circumstances and temporal resolution. Biblical intercession often connects to God's long-term purposes for justice, reconciliation, and the establishment of His kingdom on earth. This cosmic dimension enlivens the practice with hope and vision, preventing prayer from becoming merely transactional or desperate appeals. It encourages the intercessor to join the symphony of divine intention, trusting that small, faithful prayers contribute to broader spiritual movements that transcend visible outcomes. The knowledge that every whispered plea forms part of a divine mosaic infuses the intercessory journey with dignity and joy, even amid uncertainty.

The practice of intercessory prayer, when embraced with devotion and humility, shapes not only the lives of those prayed for but also the inner landscape of the intercessor. It cultivates a spirituality marked by compassion, patience, and courage. Drawing deeply from the wells of scripture and saintly example, readers are invited to envision themselves within this sacred lineage, called to bear witness to God's mercy through persistent, loving prayer. As the ancient entreaties of Moses knock at the doors of heaven and as Jesus' intimate prayers echo through eternity, contemporary believers are beckoned into a living tradition where every prayer offered on behalf of another becomes a whisper to heaven that has the power to shift hearts, open clouds, and pour out blessing.

This transformative journey is not confined to moments of prolonged solitude; it unfolds in the ordinary rhythms of life, embedded in conversations, decisions, and daily encounters. The habit of intercession teaches that prayer is not detached from reality but deeply engaged with it, a spiritual anchor that roots believers in both divine hope and earthly compassion. By nurturing this habit, readers discover an ever-deepening sense of purpose—one that connects them to the heartbeat of God and the needs of the world with tender urgency. And in this sacred engagement, intercession becomes a holy art, a channel through which the whispers of many hearts rise together, creating a chorus that resonates in heaven and on earth, bridging the human and the divine with grace and steadfast love.

Supplication: Humbly Asking for Needs

Understanding Supplication

Supplication—this tender, heartfelt cry toward the divine—holds a profound place within the vast spectrum of prayer. At its core, supplication is the earnest and humble petitioning of God, a direct appeal made from a place of vulnerability and sincere need. Unlike praise or thanksgiving, which focus on God's character or past blessings, supplication turns the gaze inward, unmasking the depths of human longing, the rawness of need, and the fragile reliance on a power far greater than oneself. To understand supplication fully is to step into a sacred dialogue where faith wrestles with uncertainty and trust embraces the unknown pathways of divine providence. It is this delicate dance of surrender and hope that the biblical narratives so poignantly unveil, inviting believers across time to carry their whispered pleas with reverence and expectancy.

In its simplest form, supplication is a form of prayer in which the supplicant openly presents their desires, fears, and needs to God. Yet, this simplicity belies a rich theological and emotional complexity. Throughout the Scriptures, supplication emerges as an act deeply woven into the fabric of a believer's spiritual life, resonating with themes of humility, dependence, and trust. To supplicate is to acknowledge one's limitations, to admit that human strength and wisdom are insufficient, and to place oneself entirely at the feet of God's sovereign will. This admission is not a defeat but a sacred act of faith—an unspoken confession that the one who listens is powerful, merciful, and intimately involved in the affairs of humanity.

The Bible presents supplication not as a mere transactional or ritualistic offering but as an authentic conversation where emotions are laid bare. Consider the psalms, where David, amid turmoil, lifts his petitions in a tone blending desperation and hope. "Hear my cry, O God; attend to my prayer" (Psalm 61:1) echo the universal need to be heard by the divine. David's supplications ripple with the tension of human frailty colliding with divine omnipotence. Through his prayers, we glimpse how supplication is a vehicle for emotional honesty, a channel through which sorrow, fear, longing, and unwavering faith converge. It is this blend of rawness and hope that defines supplicatory prayer, inviting the petitioner to trust that God's response—whether immediate or delayed—is both purposeful and caring.

Supplication also embodies a posture of reverence and submission. Biblical figures who engage in supplication often demonstrate not only the articulation of needs but also a yielding to God's greater wisdom. The prophet Daniel offers a striking example as he intercedes for his people with fervent requests, yet he concludes each petition with a submission to God's timing and will: "Hear, O our God, the prayers of your servant, and his pleas, and for the Lord's sake grant your servant success today" (Daniel 9:19). Daniel's supplication teaches a vital dimension of prayer— the humility to seek God's intervention, paired with the grace to accept divine decisions, even if outcomes diverge from personal desires. This pattern reframes supplication as an act of relational trust rather than a plea for mechanical answers.

In exploring biblical prayers of supplication, one cannot overlook the supremely instructive prayers of Jesus. In the Garden of Gethsemane, Jesus manifests the poignant dynamics of supplication as he earnestly prays, "My Father, if it is possible, let this cup pass from me; nevertheless, not as I will, but as you will" (Matthew 26:39). Here, supplication encompasses not only the expression of deep personal anguish but also the ultimate surrender to the Father's sovereign plan. Jesus' prayer reveals that supplication involves wrestling with the tension between intense desire and unconditional submission. This duality is at the heart of supplication's spiritual beauty—it creates a sacred space where human vulnerability is met with divine compassion, and where faith learns to trust in the face of uncertainty.

Supplication's place in the life of faith, therefore, extends beyond the act of asking; it encompasses the inner transformation that occurs as one draws near to God, revealing both the humility of human need and the boldness of trusting that God is attentive. The biblical writers repeatedly highlight God's attentive ear toward such prayers, portraying supplication not only as a one-sided pleading but as a dialogue where God's spirit enters into the yearning of the soul. This dynamic invites believers to consider that through supplication, they engage in a living conversation that shapes their spiritual sensitivity and openness to divine guidance.

Moreover, the practice of supplication fosters a deep sense of spiritual dependence. When the psalmists and prophets cry out for deliverance, healing, or provision, they implicitly break the illusion of self-sufficiency, embracing instead a posture where God is the sole source of hope and help. This acknowledgement is transformative—it recalibrates the heart's orientation away from the idols of control, power, and self-reliance, and places reliance on the God whose promises are steadfast. Supplication thus becomes an exercise in spiritual humility that dismantles defenses and invites a renewed awareness of God's mercy and grace.

The breadth of biblical examples further reveals that supplication is not confined to moments of crisis but is woven throughout ordinary faith journeys. Hannah's poignant prayer for a child, marked by quiet anguish and persistent hope (1 Samuel 1), exemplifies how supplication permeates the everyday desires and broken hopes of believers. Her prayer is neither adorned with grandiose language nor insincere platitudes; rather, it emanates from a heart unreservedly laid bare before God. These stories challenge contemporary believers to reclaim supplication as a vital practice—not only in dire necessity but as a habitual channel of communication that reinforces dependence and nurtures intimacy with God.

Significantly, biblical supplications often include a collective dimension. Figures such as Moses and Solomon interceded on behalf of their communities, expressing needs that transcended personal concerns. Moses, standing in the breach for Israel amid divine judgment (Exodus 32), demonstrates how supplication is also an expression of intercession, where the supplicant becomes a conduit of God's mercy for others. This communal aspect highlights the multifaceted nature of supplication, extending beyond the individual to embrace the welfare of others within the faith community. Thus, supplication binds believers not only to God but to one another, cultivating a spiritual solidarity anchored in mutual love and dependence on divine grace.

From a theological perspective, supplication intersects profoundly with the concept of God's sovereignty and providence. The biblical narrative does not portray prayer as a tool for coercing God into submission but rather as a mysterious participation in God's unfolding will. This understanding helps to harmonize the tension between prayer as request and prayer as worship; supplication becomes a means by which believers express their needs and simultaneously submit to the divine timetable and purpose. The biblical record repeatedly invites believers to trust that God's answers, whether in the form of affirmation, delay, or redirection, emerge from a perfect knowledge and love that surpass human understanding.

In practical terms, engaging in supplication requires cultivating an attitude of patience and perseverance. The parable of the persistent widow (Luke 18) illustrates that supplication is not a fleeting moment of prayer but a sustained, consistent appeal borne out of faith and hope. This portrayal encourages believers to hold fast to their petitions even when immediate responses seem absent, trusting that God's timing is perfect and that the act of persistent supplication shapes the character of the supplicant, molding resilience and deepening trust.

The emotional landscape of supplication is rich and varied, encompassing despair and hope, uncertainty and confidence, pleading and surrender. The biblical pray-ers do not sanitize their communication; rather, they reveal a full spectrum of human emotion in their appeals to God, modeling an honest, deeply relational form of prayer. This emotional candor invites contemporary believers to be genuine in their prayers, recognizing that God welcomes not only eloquence but also the simple, broken whispers of a soul in need.

Finally, supplication serves as both a safeguard against spiritual isolation and a bridge toward divine intimacy. By lifting one's needs and hopes to God, the believer enters into a profound relational exchange that nurtures spiritual growth. This exchange reorients the heart from self-centeredness to God-centeredness, cultivating a trust that God is both listening and acting. In this sacred dynamic, supplication becomes more than a request; it becomes a transformative encounter with the living God, affirming the believer's place within the divine embrace and assuring them that their cries, however faint, resonate as whispers to heaven that God hears and cherishes deeply.

Supplicatory Prayers in Scripture

Supplicatory prayers, as recorded throughout Scripture, reveal a profound dimension of human vulnerability combined with an unwavering faith in God's providence and mercy. These prayers are the whispered heart cries, the raw and earnest petitions where believers lay bare their deepest needs and desires before the Almighty, acknowledging not only their dependence but also the sovereignty of God's timing and will. Unlike prayers of praise or thanksgiving, supplicatory prayers involve a candid confession of our frailty and a hopeful entrusting of our circumstances into the hands of a loving and all-knowing Father. As we delve into the rich biblical tapestry of supplication, we are invited to witness both the humility that characterizes these prayers and the steadfast faith that undergirds them, painting a picture of a communion that is simultaneously intimate and reverent.

One of the most poignant examples of supplicatory prayer in Scripture is found in the story of Hannah, whose desperate plea in the sanctuary serves as an emblematic expression of a heart weighed down by longing and sorrow, yet lifted by hope and trust. Hannah's prayer is a sacred moment of vulnerability as she stands apart in the temple, tearfully imploring God for a child when her womb had been barren and her spirit deeply burdened. There is a rawness in her voice, a trembling earnestness in her posture, that captures the essence of supplication. Far from a mere ritual, her prayer is a sacred dialogue of heartfelt need, infused with a profound humility that acknowledges her dependence on divine intervention. The sincerity of her plea is not simply about asking for a child; it is an expression of faith that God is attentive to her sorrow and capable of transforming her barrenness into fullness. In the silence that envelops her prayer, there is both an acknowledgment of human limitation and an abiding trust in God's power to respond according to His will.

The narrative surrounding Hannah provides us with more than the mere account of petition; it invites us into the spiritual posture that marks supplicatory prayer. Her vow to dedicate her child to the Lord if her prayer is answered reflects an attitude of complete surrender and recognition that the blessing she seeks is ultimately a gift to be stewarded, not a commodity to be owned. This nuance between requesting and surrendering reveals the profound tension that believers often experience in supplication—the tension between the urgency of immediate human need and the acceptance of divine timing and purpose. Hannah's story embodies this dynamic beautifully, as her prayer transitions from the intensity of urgent pleading to the serenity of confident expectation, and finally to a life-changing testimony of God's loving faithfulness. The psalm that follows her prayer, often attributed to her, echoes this theme of both supplication and praise, reminding us that the prayer of petition is often inseparable from the praise that anticipates God's coming deliverance.

Moving from Hannah's intimate experience to the prayers uttered by Jesus himself offers a further exploration of the humility and trust inherent in supplication. Jesus, in His earthly ministry, models a prayer life marked by profound submission to the Father's will, even as He asks for relief from deeply agonizing circumstances. The Garden of Gethsemane is a sacred scene that reveals Jesus' supplicatory prayer in its most intense form—a heart wrestling with the weight of impending suffering while fully surrendering to divine sovereignty. Here, we see the true heart of supplication: a blending of honest emotional struggle with a resolute commitment to trust God's plan, no matter how frightening or onerous it might be. Jesus' prayer, "If it is possible, let this cup pass from me; yet not as I will, but as you will," encapsulates this dynamic tension beautifully. In these words, He does not shy away from expressing His desire to avoid harrowing pain; rather, He openly voices it to God, demonstrating that supplication involves both candid honesty and ultimate submission.

The prayer of Jesus in Gethsemane thus elevates our understanding of supplication by revealing that it is not a prayer of selfishness or lack of faith but a prayer of profound courage and humility. It invites believers to approach God with their deepest fears and desires, trusting that God welcomes such honesty without condemnation. The model Jesus provides quietly counters any notion that prayer must be composed of perfectly formed demands or the suppression of difficult feelings. Instead, His example reassures us that God's throne is a place for the unfiltered human heart, tender and trembling, as much as for voices lifted in praise. Moreover, Jesus' continued prayer and eventual surrender show that supplication is not a single moment but can be a process—a sustained posture of repeated presentation before the divine, especially during times of trial.

The wealth of the New Testament prayer life continues this emphasis on supplication's humility and reliance on God's timing, as the early church and apostolic writings frequently encourage believers to bring their needs before God with confidence and perseverance. The epistles teem with exhortations to offer supplications for all peoples, indicating that this form of prayer is not only personal but communal, binding the body of Christ through intercession and shared dependence on God's mercy. The Apostle Paul's prayers, notably filled with petitions for strength, wisdom, healing, and endurance, embody this reality. His willingness to reveal his own weaknesses and repeat his pleas for relief from a "thorn in the flesh" reminds us that supplication is deeply connected to the acknowledgment of human frailty and the grace that sustains even when answers are delayed or differ from expectations.

In exploring the biblical foundation of supplicatory prayer further, we see that its essence lies in a paradox—while we approach God with urgent requests born of genuine need, we do so with a spirit of surrender, recognizing God's higher wisdom and perfect timing. This tension mirrors the spiritual journey of many believers, who learn over time that supplication is as much about the transformation of the petitioner as it is about the fulfillment of requests. The act of persistent, humble prayer softens the heart, aligns the will, and deepens trust. Biblical narratives broad in scope—from Moses interceding on behalf of a rebellious people, to Solomon's plea for wisdom, to the countless cries of David through his Psalms—illustrate that supplication covers a wide emotional and situational terrain but is united by this thread of trustful dependence.

The emotional authenticity found in these biblical prayers invites readers today to reflect on their own approach to God in times of need. Supplicatory prayer is not a formulaic recitation but an intimate, dynamic conversation with God that validates our anxieties, hopes, and uncertainties. It invites honesty—whether through tears, trembling words, or silent cries—and it nurtures a relational depth that sustains the soul amidst hardship. The biblical examples teach that God meets us not with reproach but with compassion, inviting even our repeated, desperate pleas into the sacred space of divine listening. As readers meditate on these stories, they are encouraged to approach their own supplications not with fear of inadequacy but with the assurance that their whisper to heaven is heard, valued, and held by a God who is both just and merciful.

Finally, the wider biblical witness to supplicatory prayer reminds us that this sacred form of communication is accessible to all believers, past, present, and the future. It transcends the cultural and temporal distances that separate us from figures like Hannah or Jesus, bridging the ancient and modern in a timeless channel of grace. The lessons embedded within their prayers urge believers to cultivate a courageous and humble spirit, to persist in petition without losing sight of God's sovereign goodness, and to allow prayer to be a continual unfolding within their spiritual lives rather than a mere occasional appeal. This understanding opens the door to a richer prayer life—one that embraces the fragility of human experience while holding fast to the unshakable foundation of divine love. In this way, the supplicatory prayers of Scripture become not only historical records but living, breathing invitations to enter into the deepest communion with God, where our needs are met with mercy, and our hearts find solace amid life's uncertainties.

Living in Dependence Through Supplication

In the stillness of the soul, where the clamoring demands of life soften and retreat, there exists a sacred space waiting to be filled—the space of supplication. Supplication, that humble weaving of need and hope, breathes the language of our dependence, forwarding a tender yet profound narrative: that without God, we are incomplete, our hands empty, and our hearts yearning for divine grace. To live in dependence through supplication is to embrace a paradox at the heart of faith: the strength found in vulnerability and the power situated in surrender.

Many who have walked the ancient paths of scripture understood this truth deeply, allowing their prayers to unravel the threads of pride and self-sufficiency in favor of a raw, earnest reaching out toward heaven. As we explore these biblical examples, a quiet invitation unspools before us—an invitation to approach God not with demands or entitlement, but with a humility that is both a recognition of our limitations and a profound trust in the unfathomable depths of divine wisdom and timing.

Supplication arises from the recognition that we do not live by our own force or wisdom alone; it flows from the acknowledgment that our lives—fragile and fleeting as they often seem—are held within the ever-watchful hands of the Creator. When we approach God in supplication, we acknowledge that our desires, fears, and needs are not to be carried alone but entrusted to One who sees beyond the immediate horizon, whose understanding is infinite, and whose timing transcends our impatient calendars. In the biblical narrative, supplication becomes an art of delicate balance: it is both the urgent cry of the needy and the patient waiting of the faithful. Within the pages of scripture, we witness characters wrestling with their circumstances through this refined prayer, revealing to us the vulnerability that is not shameful but sacred.

Consider, for instance, the prayer of Hannah, a woman who grieved and barren, whose heartaches lead her to pour out her soul before the Lord with tears and a steadfast plea. Her supplication is not a casual request but a profound surrender, crafted out of desperation and hope entwined. She confesses her barrenness, her deep longing, and in this confession, she lays bare her soul's dependence on God's intervention. Yet despite her sorrow, Hannah's prayer is not marked by bitterness or accusation but by a trust in God's sovereignty—as she vows, quietly but firmly, that if God grants her son, she will dedicate him to His service. This act of giving herself over, even before her petition is answered, exemplifies a faith that lives amidst waiting and trusts beyond seeing. We, too, in our supplications, are called to this posture: presenting our needs honestly, yet entrusting the outcome into God's gracious hands.

Such dependence is not a sign of weakness; rather, it is a recognition of life's limits and the invitation to let God's strength undergird our frailty. The psalmist David, who knew the heights of praise and the depths of despair, frequently embodies this tension. His prayers of supplication oscillate between raw honesty and beautiful surrender: "Hear my cry, O God; attend to my prayer" (Psalm 61:1). Throughout his life, David's supplications echo with urgency and reverence, signaling that prayer is not a mechanical incantation but a living dialogue where need and trust meet. Through David's example, we observe how supplication shapes and forms a believer's heart—tearing down self-reliance and building a fortress of reliance on God's care. Therein lies a profound lesson: our cries are heard not because of their eloquence, but because they flow from a heart turned toward God with humility and unwavering faith.

The gospel reveals the ultimate example of dependence and supplication in the prayers of Jesus Himself. In the garden of Gethsemane, desperate and troubled, Jesus prays with deep agony, "Father, if it is possible, let this cup pass from me; yet not as I will, but as you will" (Matthew 26:39). Here, supplication takes on a deeply human hue—a poignant expression of desire, fear, and submission in the face of overwhelming trial. Jesus' prayer teaches us that to live in dependence is to lay bare our desires frankly before God, but also to whisper the bravest assent to the divine will. In such moments, supplication becomes a sacred surrender, a powerful act of trust woven through the fabric of divine sovereignty and human vulnerability. It is an invitation for us all to approach the Almighty, not with clenched fists demanding resolution, but with open hands and bowed hearts, willing to receive even the path we did not envision.

This attitude of humble trust stands in stark contrast to the self-sufficiency prized by our culture—a culture that often exhorts us to "pull ourselves up by our bootstraps" and meet every challenge with solo fortitude. Yet prayer, and supplication in particular, reveals the profound truth that to live well is to live connected, entwined in a web of divine care and interdependence. There is nothing shameful in admitting need; in fact, it is a spiritual grace to place ourselves vulnerably before God, admitting that without Him, we are adrift. To voice our supplications is to admit our place within a greater story—one authored by a God who is both intimately near and sovereignly vast. This is the living faith of dependence: resting in God's presence while boldly bringing our requests, confident that His timing and answer will be perfect.

The scriptures are replete with countless examples of this dynamic—the prophet Daniel fervently pleading for the restoration of his people, the apostle Paul earnestly asking God to remove his "thorn in the flesh" yet willing to receive the grace to endure, or Mary Magdalene's humble return to the resurrected Christ, open in expectation and dependence. Each narrative reinforces the delicate dance of wrestling with God in prayer, of laying bare our needs with full honesty while trusting in a love that never turns away. It is this dynamic that invites us into a richer experience of prayer—not as dry supplication or mindless repetition, but as a living conversation marked by vulnerability, persistence, and surrender.

In practical reflection, living in dependence through supplication asks us to examine the posture of our spirit as we enter prayer. Are our hearts braced with pride, hesitating to admit need? Or are they open with the wild freedom of a child who knows they belong, who cries out to their Father without fear? Do we carry in our minds the expectations and timelines we have constructed, or do we yield to God's unfolding plan with trust, even in the shadows of uncertainty? The posture of dependence invites us to cast aside illusions of control and performance, inviting us to rest deeply in God's faithfulness. In this posture, prayer blossoms into a sacred space where need becomes an offering, and waiting becomes a form of worship.

Supplication also maps out a spiritual landscape where patience and faith are inseparable companions. It is easy to pray when the answer seems immediate—the blessings fall fast, and gratitude flows naturally—but it is the endurance of prolonged silence or seeming delay that tests and refines our trust. The biblical record invites us anew to embrace these seasons, to enter the "wilderness" of waiting with the same earnest voice and open heart that first accompanied our requests. In these moments, dependence is not passive resignation, but active trust, a persistent holding on to the belief that God is at work even when unseen. We learn to whisper prayers not only of request but of hope and surrender, blending our desires with the declaration that God's will shall reign, and His timing is perfect.

Moreover, supplication weaves itself into the tapestry of community spiritual life, binding believers in collective dependence. Biblical intercession and corporate prayer reflect a shared understanding that none of us stands alone before God. Our personal needs find their place alongside the needs of others, creating a chorus of supplication that echoes God's embrace of all who seek Him. This shared journey nurtures humility—reminding us that our individual dependence is part of a larger communion where God's grace flows abundantly. To live in dependence through supplication, then, is to enter into relationship—not only with God but with the body of faith, strengthening and holding one another in prayerful reliance.

As we consider the nature of supplication, it becomes clear that this form of prayer is deeply formative, sculpting the contours of faith and character. In dependence, pride falls away and the soul grows in honesty and trust. Where the ego once demanded, the heart now waits and hopes; where anxiety grasped for control, peace plants its quiet roots. To engage daily in supplication is to cultivate this sacred rhythm—an ongoing dialogue where vulnerability is welcome, and God's faithfulness is seen anew. It is a spiritual invitation to quiet the inner tumult, unburden the soul, and lean entirely into divine compassion. In such a space, prayer ceases to be a mere task and becomes a lifeline, feeding the deep wellsprings of faith.

In embracing this posture, readers are encouraged to approach their own prayers with a softened heart and a trusting spirit. To live in dependence through supplication is to accept that our needs are known, our fears heard, and our yearnings cherished by a God who is always near. It is to adopt a prayer life that blends honesty with hope, struggle with surrender, need with trust, embodied in the biblical witness and resonant in every quiet moment of longing. This sacred practice invites us to make our whispers to heaven a continual, holy breath—an intimate conversation founded on the fragile yet profound truth that in God alone, we find our deepest life and lasting peace.

Meditative Prayer: Reflecting on God's Word

The Practice of Meditation in Prayer

To enter into the sacred rhythm of meditative prayer is to step into a timeless conversation where the soul slows, breath softens, and the heartbeat aligns with the divine pulse. Meditative prayer, far from being a silent chant or mere repetition, is a profound form of spiritual engagement that invites the believer to dwell deeply in God's presence through thoughtful reflection, attentive listening, and heartfelt openness. Rooted deeply in biblical tradition, this practice unfolds not as a hurried recital of words but as an immersive journey where the mind and spirit intertwine to ponder God's law, promises, and the mysteries of grace. It is a prayer that elevates the whispers of the heart into an echo of eternity, where scripture becomes living water, nourishing the seeker's faith and illuminating the inner landscape with divine light.

The essence of meditative prayer can be traced vividly through the Psalms and the wisdom literature, where the psalmist and sages invite us not merely to read, but to ruminate, to chew over the words of God like manna for the soul. Consider Psalm 1, which pictures the blessed man as like a tree planted by streams of water, whose delight is in the law of the Lord, and who meditates on his law day and night. Meditation here is not passive absorption; instead, it is dynamic engagement—a constant returning to God's word as a source of strength, a compass for life, and a wellspring of hope. This form of prayer embodies a deliberate, concentrated dwelling on sacred truth, allowing it to permeate one's being and transform the heart's desires and convictions. It creates a sacred space where the cacophony of daily life fades, enabling a deep attentiveness to the divine whisper that transcends words and reaches into the depths of one's very existence.

One of the most beautiful aspects of meditative prayer is its capacity to engender a profound sense of peace and intimacy with God. Unlike the urgency often found in supplicatory or intercessory prayers, meditative prayer invites stillness. Within this stillness, the believer's thoughts slow, and the spirit enters a quiet harmony, where one listens patiently and openly for the ways God might speak. This is not a passive waiting but a sacred readiness, attuned to subtle promptings and the gentle unfolding of God's presence. The meditator's heart becomes a sanctuary where divine truth is both treasured and treasured upon, cultivated intentionally through regular practice and a humble posture of receptivity. This deep communion nurtures more than intellectual knowledge; it cultivates wisdom that penetrates the core of being, fostering spiritual maturity and an ever-deepening love for the Creator.

The benefits of meditative prayer ripple beyond the moments of quiet reflection. As the practitioner trains their heart and mind to linger on God's promises and law, a spiritual transformation begins to unfold. Meditative prayer serves as a steady antidote to the fragmentation of modern life, where distractions often scatter attention and erode a sense of inner calm. By developing a disciplined practice of meditation on Scripture, believers cultivate patience and resilience, equipping themselves to navigate life's storms with grace and grounded faith. The reflective nature of meditative prayer also fosters an intimate familiarity with God's character, encouraging trust and reliance upon divine providence. It becomes a wellspring of hope in trials and a source of joy in moments of blessing, establishing a constant dialogue that renews the soul's strength day by day. This practice offers a sanctuary not just physically but spiritually, a refuge where the soul can be replenished and fortified by the holy words that speak of love, justice, mercy, and redemption.

The biblical tradition of meditation is replete with examples that reveal the transformative power of this prayer form. Moses himself embodies this contemplative posture, often retreating into the wilderness to meet with God in moments of profound silence and communion. The Torah reflects these moments, demonstrating how meditation on God's statutes was integral to maintaining covenantal faithfulness. The tradition continued in the psalms, where David's prayers weave between exultant praise and careful meditation on God's laws, illustrating prayer as a dance between heartfelt emotion and thoughtful reflection. In the New Testament, Jesus exemplifies meditative prayer in his frequent withdrawals to solitary places, where he communes deeply with the Father amid the demands of his ministry. These biblical precedents establish meditation not as a mere ascetic luxury but as an essential means of aligning the human spirit with divine will, fostering an experiential knowledge of God's presence that goes beyond words.

As meditators approach the scriptures, they practice what has been called lectio divina—a sacred reading that involves not rushing through the words but discerning their deeper meaning and allowing them to seep inward. This method invites readers to engage their entire being: the mind contemplates, the heart responds, and the will submits to the transformative power of the Word. The encounter becomes less about information and more about relationship, where God's voice resonates within the chambers of the soul. The process of meditative prayer is cyclical and participatory; it weaves together listening and responding, silence and speech, darkness and illumination. Through patient repetition and reflection, familiar passages reveal new insights, nurturing a closer friendship with God and a humbler understanding of human frailty and divine mercy.

In daily practice, meditative prayer opens pathways to spiritual sensitivity and growth. It encourages the believer to bring their whole self—thoughts, fears, hopes, and questions—into the sacred space and trust that God, who formed the heart, understands and lovingly meets every part. The rhythm of recalling God's promises can become an anchor that steadies the soul amid uncertainty, while pondering the narratives of God's faithfulness stokes the embers of faith to a steady flame. Meditation allows the texture of biblical truth to become personally relevant, knitting the ancient story into the fabric of one's lived experience. It is in these moments that prayer ceases to be a ritual and emerges as a living dialogue, a tender communion that nourishes, heals, and transforms. Meditative prayer nurtures vulnerability, inviting the soul to be fully known before God while also cultivating gratitude and awe for the mysteries that transcend human understanding.

The benefits of this sacred practice extend even further into emotional and psychological well-being. Modern research into contemplative practices echoes biblical wisdom, showing that meditation helps reduce stress, enhance emotional balance, and improve overall mental health. When rooted in prayerful meditation, these benefits take on a spiritual dimension, deepening the believer's connection to God and fostering a sense of meaning and purpose. In the quiet of meditation, faith is not only affirmed intellectually but embodied; the soul learns to rest and to trust, discovering that divine love is a steady presence in every circumstance. This sacred stillness cultivates a spaciousness within where worries give way to hope, and burdens yield to grace. The practice becomes a wellspring of resilience, equipping the faithful with the spiritual stamina to persevere when life's trials beckon.

Another profound benefit inherent in meditative prayer is the way it reshapes one's perspective on time and presence. Amid a world that often values speed and productivity, this form of prayer carves out sacred time—an intentional pause that honors the divine tempo rather than human urgency. This slow movement fosters patience and invites an ever-deepening reverence for the present moment as a bearer of divine encounter. Meditation teaches the soul to abide in God's presence without haste, recognizing that true transformation unfolds in the hush of attentiveness. In this extended communion, one begins to perceive that prayer is less about asking and more about becoming—a gradual conforming of the heart to God's will, mirroring the surrender and openness exemplified by biblical saints and by Jesus himself. The practice nurtures an abiding awareness that every moment holds the possibility of divine encounter, thus sanctifying daily life and infusing ordinary time with sacred significance.

The practice of meditative prayer also nurtures a profound humility, for it reveals the limits of human understanding and the vastness of divine mystery. As the soul ponders God's law and promises, it becomes evident that God's ways are higher than human ways, inviting trust and surrender. This humility is not a despairing admission of weakness but a freeing acknowledgment that divine grace is sufficient, and that the soul need not control or comprehend all to partake in God's goodness. Through ongoing meditation, the believer develops a sacred confidence—a faith that rests in God's faithfulness even when answers remain elusive. This trust transforms prayer from a series of requests into a dance of deepening relationship, marked by patience, hope, and a willingness to be shaped by the divine hand. Such humility also fosters greater compassion for others, as meditative prayer softens the heart and broadens the soul's capacity to embrace the brokenness of the world with empathy and intercession.

A significant dimension of meditative prayer involves the integration of the body and breath as vessels of divine encounter. While the mind contemplates scripture, the body's posture and the rhythm of breathing ground the meditator in the present moment, anchoring the spiritual journey in tangible reality. This embodiment enhances the prayer experience, reminding seekers that prayer is not a detached intellectual exercise but a holistic engagement of the entire person—body, mind, and spirit. Certain traditions within the biblical narrative reflect bodily devotion, such as the laying on of hands, kneeling, or lifting of hands toward heaven, demonstrating that physical gestures serve as outward expressions of inward attentiveness and surrender. Incorporating such embodied practices into meditation invites a fuller participation in the sacred dialogue, where the breath becomes a sacred hymn, and the body an altar upon which the soul offers its silent praises and reverent ponderings.

As meditative prayer matures, it cultivates a spirituality woven with patience, gratitude, and receptivity. It teaches the believer not merely to speak but to listen, recognizing that prayer is a two-way exchange nurtured over time through loyal devotion. The scriptures become not static words but living surfaces upon which God's presence dances and reveals new facets of truth to the attentive seeker. This dynamic interplay between divine revelation and human response enlivens the faith journey, encouraging continual growth and transformation. Meditative prayer, therefore, is a sacred apprenticeship in divine intimacy, one that shapes the heart to abide in love, reflect with wisdom, and walk in humility. The practice encourages believers to approach prayer not as an obligation but as an invitation into a mystery that is both ancient and ever new, beckoning each generation to rediscover the sacred whispers that ascend from earth to heaven.

In the final measure, to embrace meditative prayer is to embrace a way of being that nurtures communion beyond words; it is to enter a sanctuary where God's law is not a burden but a delight, where promises are not distant hopes but living realities. This form of prayer carves a path into the depths of divine-human relationship, offering a refuge amidst chaos and a compass in confusion. It nurtures the soul's capacity to trust, to hope, and to rest profoundly in God's unwavering presence. As believers engage with meditative prayer, they find themselves drawn into the biblical narrative anew, discovering that each sacred whisper, each thoughtful pause, reverberates through time and space, harmonizing their own voices with the faithful chorus of all who have sought God's face throughout the ages. It is here, in this sacred stillness, that prayer finds its truest expression—an unhurried, loving communion where the soul's softest whispers rise like incense, carried on wings of faith, ascending ceaselessly to heaven.

Biblical Foundations for Meditation

The ancient rhythms of biblical meditation echo through the corridors of Scripture as a sacred invitation—an enduring summons to draw near to the heart of God by pondering deeply His word and works. Meditation in the biblical context is not merely a ritual of repetition or a passive drifting of thoughts; rather, it is an intentional, reflective communion that engages the entire being—mind, heart, and soul—in the active consideration of God's truth. Throughout the Scriptures, this meditative practice emerges as a foundational discipline, woven into the fabric of faith itself, offering believers a transformative pathway to deepen their understanding of God, strengthen their trust in His promises, and attune their lives more closely to His divine presence.

From the earliest chapters of the Bible, the act of meditation is intimately linked with the reception and internalization of God's revelation. The psalmist's refrain, "I will meditate on your precepts and fix my eyes on your ways" (Psalm 119:15), captures the essence of this sacred reflection, where meditation becomes a deliberate focusing of the heart upon God's statutes. The Psalm 119 itself, a poetic ode to the Torah, repeatedly underscores meditation as a means to internalize God's law, allowing it to transform not only one's knowledge but the very character and conduct of the believer. Here, meditation serves as a dynamic encounter—a conversation between the individual and the divine instruction that sustains faith in fragile moments and illumines the path amid uncertainty.

The Hebrew root behind the word "meditate," often translated as "to muse" or "to mutter," suggests an intimate engagement that involves both thought and speech, a contemplative murmuring that sinks the words of God deeply into the soul. This dual action of silent rumination and vocal remembrance manifests vividly in the psalmist's practice, where meditation is both mental reflection and heartfelt surrender. The words are not merely intellectual data to be cataloged, but living waters, nourishing the spirit with the assurance of God's unfailing care. The promise found in Psalm 1 beautifully exemplifies this: "Blessed is the one who delights in the law of the Lord, and who meditates on his law day and night." Such meditation is portrayed as a continual, joyful delight—a spiritual discipline that brings life and stability, like a tree planted by streams of water, flourishing in every season.

The book of Joshua enshrines meditation as a key to obedience and success, revealing an almost practical dimension to the practice: "Keep this Book of the Law always on your lips; meditate on it day and night, so that you may be careful to do everything written in it. Then you will be prosperous and successful" (Joshua 1:8). This passage highlights meditation not as an isolated, passive exercise but as the conduit through which divine guidance becomes manifest in concrete action. The meditative pondering of the law cultivates a profound intimacy with God's will, a readiness that arms the believer against the distractions of the world and aligns decision-making with heavenly wisdom. Thus, biblical meditation operates as both spiritual nourishment and strategic preparation—an ancient wisdom for living faithfully amid the complexities of existence.

Beyond the legalistic or moral framework, meditation in Scripture frequently encompasses the marveling at God's creative works and mighty deeds, enriching the believer's sense of awe and gratitude. The Psalms, in particular, invite the faithful to meditate on the wonders of God's handiwork, as in Psalm 143:5: "I remember the days of old; I meditate on all your works and consider what your hands have done." This form of meditation shifts the gaze from inward reflection on the law to outward contemplation of God's ongoing activity in history and nature. Such reflection awakens a vibrant awareness of God's sustaining and redemptive power, inviting believers to see their lives within the sweeping narrative of divine providence. Here, meditation transcends mere textual study to become a worshipful encounter, a spiritual attentiveness to the traces of God's presence in the world around us.

Within the wisdom literature, meditation finds a nuanced expression as an intellectual and spiritual discipline that harmonizes human understanding with divine revelation. Proverbs exhorts the believer to treasure wisdom as one would precious jewels and to "ponder the path of your feet; then all your ways will be sure" (Proverbs 4:26). This form of meditation entails careful, deliberate reflection on life's choices in conformity with God's wisdom. As such, meditation fosters discernment and prudence, enabling believers to navigate the complexities of life with clarity and peace. In the same thread, Ecclesiastes threatens the folly of ignoring God's holy law and encourages thoughtful consideration of the brevity and meaning of life (Ecclesiastes 7:25). This contemplative posture underscores the biblical understanding that meditation is inseparable from the pursuit of wisdom and the fear of the Lord—a reverent acknowledgement that deepens the roots of authentic spirituality.

The prophetic books, too, reinforce meditation as a vital spiritual practice, often linking it with hearing God's voice and responding in faithfulness. Jeremiah, for example, speaks of the word of God as a fire within his heart, one that cannot be contained but must be pondered and proclaimed (Jeremiah 20:9). Such meditation is an active wrestling with divine revelation, where the prophet's inner turmoil mirrors a faithful entanglement with the mysterious plans of God. Isaiah's vision of the Lord in the temple (Isaiah 6) calls for a reflective response, a meditative encounter that leads to commissioning and transformation. The prophets invite readers not only to listen but to meditate on the implications of God's word for personal and communal transformation—an engagement that requires vulnerability, courage, and unwavering attention.

The New Testament continues this rich heritage of meditation, encouraging believers to immerse themselves in the teachings and person of Jesus Christ as the ultimate revelation of God's love and truth. The Apostle Paul exhorts the church to set their minds on whatever is true, noble, right, pure, lovely, and admirable, instructing that such meditation fosters the peace of God that transcends all understanding (Philippians 4:8-9). This passage indicates a meditative discipline that sanctifies thought itself, transforming the mental landscape in alignment with heavenly virtues. The epistle to the Hebrews encourages believers to hold fast to their confession and to consider Jesus, the pioneer and perfecter of faith (Hebrews 12:2), inviting a meditative gaze fixed on the character and mission of Christ, which strengthens perseverance in trials and nurtures spiritual vitality.

Within the Gospels, Jesus himself exemplifies meditative prayer, especially in His moments of solitude and communion with the Father. His often solitary withdrawal to pray and His reflective engagement with Scripture suggest a model for meditative practice that balances active ministry with contemplative silence. Jesus' prayer in the Garden of Gethsemane, marked by honest wrestling with divine will, reveals the profound emotional and spiritual dimensions of contemplative prayer—an openness to God's purposes that embraces both surrender and petition. The Lord's Prayer, offered as a model, encapsulates various types of prayer, but its rhythm and focus invite meditative repetition and deep reflection upon God's name, kingdom, and will. Through Jesus' example, meditation becomes a way to embody trust, submission, and intimate dialogue with the divine.

The epistles further expand meditation as a communal and personal discipline that shapes the believer's life and character. Paul's instruction to Timothy to devote himself to the public reading, exhortation, and teaching (1 Timothy 4:13) implies a meditative preparation on God's word, shaping effective ministry through thoughtful internalization. Peter admonishes believers to desire the pure milk of the word so that they may grow spiritually (1 Peter 2:2), suggesting a patient, reflective nourishment akin to meditation. These pastoral exhortations underscore meditation as an essential practice for spiritual maturity and the deepening of faith, opening the heart to the sanctifying work of the Spirit.

Moreover, biblical meditation is not confined to an individual or intellectual exercise; it is a spiritual discipline that transforms perception and informs action. The Psalms frequently link meditation with praise, declaring that those who meditate on God's law will be blessed and prosper (Psalm 1:2-3), framing meditation as a joyful engagement that yields flourishing in life and faith. This dynamic interplay between reflection and life points to meditation as a pilgrimage inward and outward—an exploration of the divine mysteries that invigorates the believer's witness and service in the world. The meditative life, therefore, is marked by a continuous cycle of listening, pondering, responding, and living out the word of God in tangible ways.

The historical context of biblical meditation also reveals its communal significance. In the daily rhythm of Israel's worship, meditation on the Torah was central to forming a covenant identity, teaching successive generations the sacred narrative that shaped their existence. This meditative engagement with Scripture cultivated a shared spirituality grounded in memory and hope, anchoring the community amid exile, conquest, and renewal. The Psalms functioned as communal prayers and songs, inviting the faithful to join in corporate meditation upon God's works—expressing lament, praise, thanksgiving, and trust. Such communal meditation enhances the experience of solidarity and mutual encouragement, reminding believers that prayerful contemplation is never an isolated endeavor but a shared journey into the heart of God.

In contemporary practice, drawing from these biblical foundations enhances personal meditation by rooting it in the living tradition of faith. Meditative prayer, modeled on ancient biblical patterns, invites a posture of attentive listening—where the believer opens their heart to receive the whispers of God, allowing His word to dwell richly within them. This practice can involve slow, intentional reading of Scripture, accompanied by silent reflection, repetition of key verses, or imaginative engagement with biblical scenes, thereby invoking the imaginations, emotions, and intellects as instruments of divine encounter. By following this biblical example, meditation becomes a dynamic dialogue, engaging not only the mind but also the whole person in worshipful communion.

The promises of God, often meditated upon in Scripture, also serve as a wellspring for hope and resilience, particularly amid trials. The psalmist's frequent recourse to God's steadfast love and faithfulness provides a repository of divine assurances to draw upon in moments of doubt and despair. Reflecting on these promises in meditation becomes an act of faith, anchoring the believer's soul in the unchanging character of God. Similarly, the New Testament's emphasis on the assurance of salvation, the indwelling Spirit, and the hope of resurrection enriches the meditative journey, nurturing a confident trust that transcends temporal circumstances.

In essence, biblical meditation is an integrative discipline that embraces the complexity of human spirituality—thought and feeling, intellect and intuition, worship and obedience. It is a holistic way of encountering God, inviting believers to dwell deeply in His presence and to allow His word to shape their inner and outer lives. Meditation calls for a slowing down of the hurried pace of life, a turning aside into sacred quiet where the noise of the world recedes, and the voice of God becomes discernible. The faithful who embrace this practice find themselves drawn into an ancient yet ever-new rhythm, where the whispers of heaven become audible and transformative.

Ultimately, the biblical foundations for meditation impress upon us a profound truth: meditation is both a gift and a discipline that nurtures intimacy with God, aligning our hearts with His eternal purposes. It invites believers into a sacred dialogue where reflection births transformation, and where the mind's engagement with Scripture opens a pathway into the mystery of divine love. As we follow the biblical calls to meditate on God's word and works, we discover that prayer is not confined to fleeting moments but becomes a continuous whisper to heaven, a steady flame illuminating the soul's deepest longing for communion with the Creator. This ancient practice, rooted in Scripture's sacred narrative, equips us today to walk the path of faith with renewed hope, steadfast courage, and abiding peace.

Applying Meditation Today

In the quiet moments of life, when the world's clamor falls away and a stillness takes hold, the practice of meditation finds its sacred space, inviting the soul to wander deeper into the heart of God's presence. Applying meditation within our prayer life is not merely a technique to achieve calm or clarity; rather, it is an intentional journey into the profound mystery of divine communion. This ancient rhythm, deeply rooted in the biblical tradition, calls us to linger with Scripture—pondering its weight and melody—as an act of worship and transformation. Meditation in prayer is a gentle yet powerful conduit through which the whisper of heaven reaches the depths of our being, reshaping our thoughts, expectations, and even our very spirits.

Embracing meditative prayer today begins with cultivating an environment where such divine dialogue can flourish. In the midst of our fast-paced, distracted world, setting aside intentional time and space feels almost revolutionary. Yet, it is this very intentionality that opens the doorway. Find a place that nurtures silence—not merely the absence of external noise, but the fostering of inner stillness. This could be a corner of your room adorned with a candle or a simple cross, a bench in a quiet park, or even a moment stolen in the early morning before dawn's light stretches across the sky. The significance lies not in grandeur but in sacredness—transformed by your reverence and openness. Begin by quieting the restless mind. This might take breathing deeply, letting the body relax into the subtle pulse of life, or perhaps briefly speaking a prayer inviting God's Spirit to settle within. The act of preparing the heart—creating a sanctuary within and without—is a foundational step toward entering meditation as a prayerful posture.

Once the space is sanctified by gentle silence, meditation invites the sacred text to take center stage, not as a checklist of verses to be conquered or analyzed but as a living word to be absorbed and tasted slowly. The biblical tradition offers a sumptuous feast to ponder: the promises of God's steadfast love, the intricate wisdom of the psalms, the tender petition of Hannah's prayer, or the serene submission of Jesus in Gethsemane. Let the chosen passage or promise wash over your consciousness. Read or recite it slowly, savor each word as if it carries a fragrance that lingers in the air. You might read the passage aloud softly or whisper it beneath your breath, allowing the cadence and rhythm of the ancient language, or its modern translation, to echo within. At times, silence will naturally fall between repetitions, inviting your spirit to grapple or embrace the mystery contained in the text.

The heart of meditative prayer lies in pondering. This pondering is not a hurried reflection but a sustained dwelling in God's presence, a deliberate soaking that nurtures both faith and personal transformation. Bring your whole self to this reflection—mind, emotions, body, and soul. Let your thoughts rest gently on the meaning, implications, and comfort of the words. Does the passage stir feelings of hope or sorrow? Does it convict gently or encourage boldly? Is there a particular phrase that seems to shimmer with special light today? These moments of reflection allow the Word to speak personally, softly breaking through any hardened layers within, inviting healing, reassurance, or a call to action. The meditative aspect is dynamic; sometimes your thoughts will gently follow the flow of Scripture, and at others, a deeper silence will settle over your heart, creating space for God's Spirit to move in ways beyond words.

To incorporate meditation into daily prayer life effectively, it may be helpful to use a flexible rhythm rather than a strict routine, allowing space for the Spirit to lead. Perhaps begin each session with a brief prayer of surrender, inviting God to lead your meditation, followed by slowly reading a short passage. Then, rest in silence, giving time to the inner reflections that rise naturally. Journal your thoughts and impressions afterward, capturing the whispers that sometimes elude memory. Over time, this practice becomes a sacred dialogue, where prayer is no longer a one-way communication but a living two-way exchange. Each session becomes a step deeper into spiritual intimacy, where the Word of God is not only heard but becomes life-giving water to the thirsty soul.

Guided meditation can also enrich this practice, especially for those newer to meditative prayer. Listening to a recorded Scripture reading or a prayerful reflection can help anchor your heart when wandering thoughts crowd the mind. Additionally, focusing on a single word or phrase from the Scripture, such as "peace," "hope," or "trust," can serve as a mantra, continually drawing your attention back to divine truths when distractions arise. Yet, the power of meditative prayer is not in repetition alone, but in openness—allowing not only your voice but God's voice to shape the encounter. Be patient with the process; the quiet unfolding of meditative prayer often defies our urge for immediate understanding or feeling. It is a long breath of spiritual attentiveness, a holy listening that may first appear subtle but gradually reshapes the contours of our inner landscape.

Meditation in prayer invites us to enter the biblical tradition of "chewing" on God's law and promises, as the psalmist so poignantly illustrates in Psalm 1:2, where delighting in the law of the Lord and meditating on it day and night becomes the wellspring of life and vitality. This image of chewing provokes a tactile spirituality—one that demands time, patience, and continual engagement. The biblical figures were not merely readers or hearers of God's word; they were ponderers, carriers of divine truth who let it transform their identity and actions. In our practice, then, meditation becomes more than mental exercise; it is a transformative encounter that seeps into daily living, reshaping how we respond to suffering, joy, and uncertainty with a spirit rooted deeply in God's faithfulness.

A practical aspect to consider when adopting meditation is the recognition that this form of prayer is not reserved for rare moments of profound solitude. It can be woven into the fabric of daily life: in quiet moments during a lunch break, as a refuge in the morning rush, or an anchor in the evening's stillness. Key to this integration is intentionality—choosing to pause and listen rather than moving relentlessly into busyness. Creating rituals around these pauses can foster both spiritual rhythm and resilience. Lighting a candle, opening a Bible to a familiar passage, or gently closing the eyes can function as signals to the soul that a sacred moment is commencing. These physical acts help train the body and mind to slow down, inviting the whole person into the meditative space.

Incorporating breath into meditative prayer adds another dimension of bodily intimacy to the process of communing with God. Breath, the essential thread of life woven into both human and spiritual rhythms, can serve as a bridge—a reminder of God's sustaining presence in every moment. Practitioners often find it helpful to synchronize their breathing with the phrases of Scripture or prayers. For example, inhaling deeply while silently saying, "The Lord is my" and exhaling slowly with "shepherd; I shall not want." This rhythmic breathing deepens focus and roots the meditation in the embodied experience of the present moment. It becomes a prayer not only of the mind but of the body, who, in its very breathing, testifies to the goodness and nearness of God.

One of the blessings of this practice lies in its extraordinary accessibility. There is no formula to perfect or hierarchical standard to meet; meditation is a sacred gift extended to all seekers across the ages. What differs is the way each person meets God in this silence and slow reflection, shaped by personality, circumstances, and spiritual maturity. For the restless or the anxious, meditation offers a calming refuge, an anchor against the storm of distraction and worry. For the weary or afflicted, it opens a chamber where God's soothing presence can be felt as balm. For the joyful and hopeful, meditation becomes a way to steep more deeply in gratitude, extending the heart toward the source of all goodness. No matter one's season or struggle, this practice stands ready to meet the soul's diverse needs with tenderness and profound grace.

Yet, it is essential to acknowledge that meditation also brings vulnerability. As we slow and open, often unsettling emotions or unexamined fears may arise. Just as biblical lament emerges through the rawness of honest prayer, meditative prayer invites us to hold whatever surfaces with loving attention, without judgment or hurried escape. It is naturally a process of encounter—sometimes with joy, sometimes with sorrow, always with God. Such vulnerability is itself a form of holiness, teaching us to trust the divine embrace beyond our control, even in the depths of uncertainty. Thus, meditation prepares not only the mind but the heart for deeper faith and resilience, helping us bear the full spectrum of human experience while resting securely in God's unwavering love.

As meditative prayer deepens, it often opens the way to contemplative silence, the sacred space where words begin to fall away, and pure presence addresses pure presence. This silent communion is a mystical dimension of prayer—an encounter with God that transcends language and access the Divine Mystery in shared stillness. In this silence, meditation becomes a sanctuary where time itself seems to pause, and the soul drinks deeply from the well of divine grace. Engaging regularly with this silent dimension can nurture a profound sense of peace and spiritual renewal, a reminder that prayer is more than speech; it is the sacred dance of presence and response that forms the heart of all true communion.

Encouraging the practice of Christian meditation in contemporary life also involves integrating communal experiences. Though often pursued privately, meditative prayer can be enriched within worship gatherings or small groups, where shared silence and Scripture reflections foster both solidarity and deeper insight. Listening to the diverse ways others experience and articulate their meditation can illuminate fresh facets of Scripture and common longing, forging bonds of spiritual kinship. This communal dimension reminds us that, though prayer is intimate, it is also rooted in the Body of Christ—participants united across time and space in the same sacred whisper to heaven. Sharing these moments aids in overcoming isolation and enriches the spiritual journey with accountability and encouragement.

The transformative power of meditation in prayer does not rest solely in the quiet moments themselves but in the fruit that flows outward into daily living. Meditative prayer shapes how one sees the world, making room for grace and wisdom in decisions, relationships, and responses to life's challenges. By returning again and again to God's Word in meditation, believers cultivate a lens of divine love and truth through which the complexity and brokenness of the world can be met with hope and courage. Meditation roots the soul firmly in the promises of God, ensuring that faith does not remain abstract but bursts forth in acts of kindness, justice, and peace. The prayer of meditation thus becomes a wellspring from which life flows, offering sustenance and strength for the long journey of discipleship.

Finally, to truly apply meditation today, cultivate patience and gentleness with oneself. Spiritual growth is seldom linear, and the quest for stillness can meet resistance—from restless thoughts to external demands. Approach the practice with an open heart and without self-condemnation. If the mind wanders, gently guide it back to the sacred word or your breath, recognizing that each return is itself an act of faithful prayer. Embrace the unfolding mystery of meditation as a sacred gift unfolding in its own time. Keep a spirit of curiosity rather than urgency, allowing each meditative session to be a unique encounter shaped by both God's timing and your readiness. Through such compassionate persistence, meditation blossoms from a disciplined technique into a treasured practice that deepens your prayer life, enriches your spiritual journey, and fills your days with the enduring whispers of heaven.

Spiritual Warfare: Prayers for Protection and Strength

Understanding Spiritual Warfare

In the shadowed recesses of human experience, where unseen battles rage beyond the perception of our senses, prayer emerges as a flaming sword, a divine bulwark wielded against the forces that threaten our spiritual well-being. Understanding the nature of spiritual warfare is not merely an abstract theological exercise but a vital step toward embracing prayer as a potent means of defense and courage in the face of adversity. When the biblical narratives whisper to us about the seen and unseen realms, we are beckoned into a reality that transcends flesh and bone, a realm where angels struggle with principalities and powers, where the mind is a battlefield, and where every utterance of prayer can shift the tides of cosmic conflict.

At the heart of spiritual warfare lies the acknowledgment of a relentless adversary, one who prowls and schemes to unseat the believer from the fortress of faith. The Bible reveals this adversary not as a mythic figure cloaked in darkness alone but as a cunning, patient force intent on distortion and destruction. Our prayers, therefore, become more than supplications—they transform into declarations of divine authority and protection. When David cried out for deliverance from his foes or when the apostles prayed for boldness amidst persecution, they were not simply communicating with God; they were engaging in a spiritual campaign to dismantle the strongholds that threatened them. Their prayers embodied resistance, a spiritual vigilance that recognized the enemy's tactics and invoked the power of heaven to counter them.

These ancient battles waged through prayer invite today's believer to wake from any slumber of complacency. The struggle is not against visible enemies alone but against forces that seek to divert the soul's destiny through deceit, fear, and oppression. Spiritual warfare prayers thus carry an urgency—a cry for armor, shield, and sword—to withstand the fiery darts launched against faith and hope. Yet, they also embody courage, drawing from the reservoir of God's promises that no weapon formed against us shall prosper. The prayers of protection articulate a deep trust in divine sovereignty, acknowledging that while external circumstances may swirl in chaos, the inward life secured by God's presence remains unshaken.

Moreover, these prayers are rich tapestries woven with both boldness and humility, invoking the name of Jesus as a refuge while recognizing the believer's own vulnerability. They remind us that spiritual warfare is not fought in human strength but in surrendered reliance on God's power. The Apostle Paul exhorts believers to put on the whole armor of God, describing each piece—belt of truth, breastplate of righteousness, helmet of salvation, shield of faith, sword of the Spirit, and the readiness of the gospel of peace—not as metaphorical niceties but as essential elements in the believer's prayer life. This imagery invites us to see prayer itself as a dynamic engagement, a continual posture of readiness and resistance through spoken word, meditation, and invocation.

Yet, the biblical record does not depict spiritual warfare prayers solely as defensive postures; they also reveal a proactive embrace of spiritual authority. When Moses interceded for the people in the wilderness or when Jesus rebuked the demonic forces openly, prayer functioned as a declaration of God's reign breaking in, a reversal of the dominion of darkness. This dimension imbues our prayers with a dual character: one of seeking refuge and one of advancing the kingdom. Our petitions for protection carry the implicit demand that evil release its claim, that darkness be exposed and overcome by the light. Therein lies a profound mystery of prayer's potency—that through words spoken in faith, the unseen spiritual realm is realigned in accordance with God's will.

Understanding spiritual warfare also involves an appreciation of the emotional and psychological terrain upon which these battles are fought. The Bible is candid about the weariness, fear, and despair that often accompany such struggles, and the prayers of protection resonate with this raw honesty. The psalms, in particular, offer vivid portrayals of anguish and plea for deliverance, capturing the tumult of spiritual conflict with unvarnished candor. These prayers teach us that spiritual warfare is not a sanitized, heroic narrative; it is filled with moments of doubt and vulnerability where the soul cries out for rescue and strength. Such prayers affirm that lament and fear have their sacred place in the dialogue with God, preparing the way for courage to be renewed.

Furthermore, the protective prayers modeled in Scripture reveal the importance of communal support in spiritual warfare. Intercessory prayer, when believers join together to stand against the forces of evil, amplifies the power of petition. This collective wage war in the invisible realm reflects the biblical vision of the body of Christ as a united front, where the prayers of many can break chains and fortify the weak. The stories of the early church's prayers under persecution depict vibrant examples of this spiritual solidarity, inviting modern readers to embrace not just individual but corporate prayer as a source of strength and protection.

In the modern world, filled with its myriad distractions and spiritual challenges, grasping the realities of spiritual warfare through prayer is profoundly relevant. The noise and chaos of contemporary life can obscure the solemnity and urgency of this unseen battle, yet it is here that prayer becomes a sanctuary and a sword. It enables believers to navigate trials with steady hearts, drawing courage not from circumstance but from the steadfast presence of God. These prayers for protection are not invocations of escapism but affirmations of engagement, a refusal to be passive in the face of spiritual assault, and a commitment to stand firm in God's victorious power.

As readers step into this sacred understanding, they are invited to cultivate a prayer life that is alert, intentional, and fearless. Prayer becomes a rhythm of spiritual readiness, where each moment is an opportunity to put on divine armor, each word a declaration of faith, and each breathing moment an act of trust. The Bible's depiction of spiritual warfare reveals that prayer is not simply a last resort but the frontline in the believer's journey, a holy dialogue where human fragility meets divine strength and where whispered words ascend to heaven and bring forth peace amidst battle.

In embracing this truth, the complexities of spiritual warfare take shape not as a source of terror but as an invitation into the transforming power of God's presence. Through prayer, the believer becomes a participant in a cosmic drama, a bearer of light in shadowed realms, and a vessel of courage amid unseen storms. The prayers of protection serve as a testament to the ever-present reality that while the battles may be fierce and the enemy relentless, the God who listens is more powerful still. This understanding thus empowers readers to see their own prayers not as mere habit or ritual but as divine weapons and shields, crafted by grace and wielded with faith, echoing the timeless whispers to heaven that pierce the darkness with hope and victory.

Biblical Prayers for Defense

The ancient scriptures echo with the fervent voices of those who, amid trials and tribulations, sought refuge in the divine fortress of God. Prayers for defense offer a profound window into the human encounter with spiritual warfare, portraying not only the threat of visible adversaries but also the unseen battles waged within and beyond. In these sacred appeals, we discover a vibrant tapestry woven with trust and trembling, courage and supplication, where the supplicant turns to God's mighty hand as shield and sword in times of peril. This sacred dialogue is timeless, revealing how prayer becomes a sanctuary, a spiritual bulwark that empowers, protects, and transforms.

One of the earliest and most vivid examples of a prayer begging for divine protection unfolds in the life of Moses, a figure whose leadership was carved in the wilderness, fraught with opposition both external and internal. When the Israelites faced the encroaching armies of Amalek, it was Moses who lifted his hands in desperate intercession—his raised hands an emblem of heavenly petition and earthly weariness alike. The people's survival hinged on his perseverance in prayer, a powerful metaphor reminding us that defense in the spiritual realm depends not only on human strength but on sustaining an unyielding connection to the divine. This scene captures prayer as an active and communal endeavor; Moses' hands faltered only when support waned, illustrating how collective faith and shared spiritual vigilance can bolster the individual's prayer for protection. God's intervention when Moses' hands remained raised signals prayer's efficacy in spiritual warfare—a vivid reminder that God's shield is responsive to enduring faith.

King David, whose life was a mosaic of valor and vulnerability, offers some of the most poignant prayers for defense recorded in the Psalms. His cries to God resonate from caves of hiding and battlefields alike, wearing the raw honesty of a soul besieged by enemies visible and unseen. His request for God to be a "shield around me"—a phrase repeated across the Psalms—conjures the image of divine armor clasped tightly around the believer's frailty, imbuing him with supernatural courage. Yet David's prayers are not mere invocations for physical safety; they express a profound yearning for moral and spiritual preservation amid temptation and despair. He seeks God's defense not only against external assaults but also to guard his heart from the corrosive forces of fear, doubt, and sin. Within these prayers, the interplay between divine protection and human surrender reveals the nuanced dynamic of spiritual defense, where reliance on God becomes the very source of a warrior's strength.

Beyond these well-trod narratives, the Book of Daniel presents another remarkable testimony to prayer as a means of divine defense against spiritual adversaries. Daniel's prayer in the lion's den, steeped in unwavering confidence and humility, unfolds as an extraordinary act of trust in God's sovereign shield. His calm amidst the teeth of danger articulates a profound truth: that the power of prayer transcends physical circumstance, offering a sanctuary for the soul that guards it even when the body appears vulnerable. Daniel's faith is not a shield that repels danger by force but one that transforms the very nature of the threat, rendering the lions' teeth powerless. In this, prayer becomes less a call for physical invincibility and more a plea for spiritual invulnerability—a divine presence that watches, protects, and ultimately delivers.

The New Testament deepens this vision of prayer for defense by framing spiritual warfare as an ongoing internal and external conflict against forces of darkness. The Apostle Paul, in his epistle to the Ephesians, exhorts believers to "put on the full armor of God" and to "pray in the Spirit on all occasions with all kinds of prayers and requests." Paul's instructions emphasize prayer not as a solitary shield but as a dynamic part of spiritual armor, complementing faith, righteousness, and salvation. He paints a vivid picture of the believer standing firm against "the devil's schemes," suggesting that defensive prayer is both protective and proactive. It nurtures spiritual readiness, fortifies inner strength, and invites divine empowerment that transcends human capacity. Through Paul's writings, prayer emerges as a relentless presence in the battlefield of the spirit, weaving together supplication, vigilance, and resilience.

One particular prayer attributed to Paul encapsulates this essence when he pleads for boldness to proclaim the Gospel amid opposition, asking God to "open my mouth" and to guard him from harm. This prayer underscores the dual nature of defense prayers: they seek physical protection, yes, but more importantly, they ask for spiritual courage and the safeguarding of faith under fire. Paul's vulnerability and strength dance together poignantly, inviting contemporary believers to recognize that seeking God's shield is not a sign of weakness but a declaration of dependence on divine grace amid life's many battles. In the complex warfare between the seen and unseen, prayer serves as a sanctified strategy, a spiritual weapon that disarms fear and uproots hopelessness.

Likewise, the prayers of Jesus Himself cast a luminous model of defense prayer, blending submission and boldness in a sacred dance of dependency and triumph. In the Garden of Gethsemane, Jesus offers a prayer soaked in anguish yet crowned by surrender: "Father, if you are willing, take this cup from me; yet not my will, but yours be done." This prayer is a sublime exemplar of spiritual defense, not through avoidance of suffering but through embracing the divine will even in the face of impending torment. It reveals prayer as the ultimate fortress, not shielding from hardship but transforming the heart so that fear loses its grip and courage finds its home in God's presence. By praying for deliverance tempered with willing surrender, Jesus models a potent defense—one that does not resist the thrust of affliction but invites God's strength to prevail amid it.

Moreover, in His high priestly prayer recorded in the Gospel of John, Jesus prays for His followers' protection from "the evil one," asking God to "keep them safe by the power of your name." This intercessory prayer embraces the divine shield as an active force, a power wrought in God's name that both guards and empowers believers against the forces arrayed against them. Here, prayer transcends personal defense and becomes communal, extending blessings of protection to others, illustrating the expansive reach of prayer as a spiritual bulwark. It challenges readers to see defense prayer not merely as a personal fortress but as a shared shield resting on the shoulders of a faithful community.

The epistle of James offers another dimension, emphasizing the power of prayer to resist the devil and to resist temptation. James writes that "the prayer of a righteous person is powerful and effective," highlighting the integral role of prayer in spiritual resistance. This gives rise to an understanding of defense prayers not just as requests for external intervention but as spiritual disciplines that bolster moral fortitude and inner vigilance. Winning the battle thus requires more than physical armaments; it demands an internal strengthening through prayer that steadies the soul and aligns the heart with God's protection.

Throughout these examples, a recurring theme emerges: prayer for defense is never merely a petition for physical safety or the avoidance of conflict. Rather, it is an acknowledgment of human vulnerability and a transcendence toward divine strength. It is the recognition that true defense arises when the soul is fortified, and the spirit is armored by unshakable faith. This faith is not passive but active, grappling with fear, enduring anguish, confronting enemies—both tangible and invisible— and emerging resilient through the power of God's presence.

The psalms, a treasury of poetic prayers, frequently return to the motif of God as a refuge and shield. They paint pictures of God as a fortress impregnable, a rampart against the storm. Psalm 91, for instance, is a luminous hymn of trust that vividly declares God's protection from "the snare of the fowler" and "deadly pestilence." The psalmist's words are drenched in assurance, inviting those who pray to cling to God's promises as a shield that withstands the chaos of life's dangers. These prayers encapsulate the emotional landscape of defense prayer—moving through fear, assurance, and peace—offering the reader an intimate doorway into whispered conversations with the divine where courage is renewed, and the soul finds its stronghold.

Notably, the act of praying for defense often involves a surrender that paradoxically empowers. The recognition of humans as fragile and finite compels a reliance on God, and through this dependence, the believer finds a strength unattainable by self alone. These prayers reveal an intricate dance between acknowledging weakness and embracing God's omnipotence. The repeated invocation of God as "rock," "shield," and "refuge" punctuates the biblical narrative with a rhythmic assurance that even when walls crumble, the believer's heart can remain steadfast because it is anchored in the eternal.

In practical terms, the prayers for defense outlined in the Bible invite readers into a rich tradition that validates their own struggles and fears while pointing toward a divine source of strength. They offer a spiritual template that moves beyond rote repetition, encouraging a heartfelt, honest engagement with God. Whether facing the tangible challenges of persecution, illness, or hardship, or wrestling with the invisible foes of doubt, despair, and temptation, these prayers provide a vocabulary and a vision—a way to articulate the deep-seated yearning for protection and courage.

The biblical landscape also reminds readers that defense through prayer is never completely solitary. It involves community, encouragement, and solidarity. The collective prayers of the faithful—whether in the form of Moses' upheld hands, the communal cries in the Psalms, or the early church's united prayers—highlight the power of shared spiritual striving. In times of spiritual warfare, this community becomes a living, breathing fortress of intercession, each voice reinforcing another, weaving a net of divine protection that reaches across both time and space.

Engaging with these biblical prayers for defense, modern readers are invited to draw courage not only from the words themselves but from the lives behind them—the kings, prophets, apostles, and the Savior—whose faith trembled yet stood firm. Such prayers beckon readers to make their own whispers of plea and praise, weaving their vulnerabilities with divine strength in a sacred tapestry that connects the ancient to the present. In doing so, prayer becomes not simply a practice but a lifeline in the spiritual battles that every believer faces, a radiant shield that wards off despair and kindles hope.

Ultimately, the prayers for defense in the Bible carry more than instructions; they transmit a spiritual posture marked by courage suffused with humility, power mingled with trust. They affirm that while struggles may be relentless and enemies formidable, the believer's ultimate security rests in a God who neither slumbers nor fades. These prayers nurture a resilient heart capable of facing storms and shadows, inviting the faithful to stand firm, shielded and emboldened by divine love. Through this sacred dialogue, each whisper to heaven becomes a living shield, a beacon of courage, and a promise of peace amid the unceasing warfare of the soul.

Engaging in Spiritual Warfare Prayer

In the vast and often turbulent realm of the spiritual life, prayer emerges not merely as a gentle whisper but as a clarion call — a profound weapon wielded with faith, courage, and unwavering conviction. To engage in spiritual warfare through prayer is to step boldly into a sacred battle that transcends human sight and earthly conflict, embracing a confrontation that touches the very heart of divine mystery and cosmic struggle. The Bible presents prayers of spiritual warfare not only as acts of defense but as declarations of divine truth piercing the veils of doubt, fear, and temptation that seek to ensnare the soul. When believers engage in this sacred practice, they are invited to stand firm with the whole armor of God, placing on the belt of truth, the breastplate of righteousness, feet shod with readiness to bear the gospel of peace, the shield of faith to quell the fiery darts of the evil one, the helmet of salvation, and the sword of the Spirit, which is the word of God. Each element becomes emblematic not only of protection but of proactive engagement, symbolizing the intimate connection between prayer and spiritual readiness.

Prayer in spiritual warfare is not a last resort nor a timid appeal; it is a deliberate, potent act of faith that confronts forces often unseen but deeply felt. It acknowledges the reality of spiritual opposition yet rejects its dominion, trusting in the sovereignty of God over every realm. The psalmist's cries for deliverance resonate powerfully here, as does the bold intercession of the apostle Paul, who exhorts believers to "Pray at all times in the Spirit, with all prayer and supplication" so that they may stand firm against "the schemes of the devil." This exhortation unveils prayer's dynamic nature — a relentless, ongoing engagement, a resistance illuminated not by sheer human willpower but by the Spirit's empowerment. The spiritual warrior's prayer is layered with urgency and reverence, combining lament over the trials and temptations that assail the faithful with jubilant praise for God's steadfast presence and ultimate victory.

To pray boldly in the context of spiritual warfare is to lay bare the soul without fear or reservation, acknowledging both human vulnerability and divine strength. It is a confession of dependence on God amidst the chaos, a firm refusal to succumb to despair or silence. The prayers of the prophets, such as Elijah, who faced opposition with fiery resolve undergirded by profound trust, offer vivid models. When Elijah prayed on Mount Carmel, his words shattered the silence of doubt and called down fire from heaven — a miraculous affirmation of divine authority through the conduit of fervent prayer. Likewise, Daniel's prayers in the lion's den, saturated with humility and perseverance, exemplify the subtler but equally potent spiritual warfare conducted in moments of quiet courage. These biblical examples teach that spiritual warfare prayer is not always loud or dramatic; often, it is the concealed, steadfast crying to God that forms the backbone of spiritual resistance.

The courage embodied in spiritual warfare prayer comes from deep within the believer's spiritual reservoir — a wellspring replenished continually by scripture, meditative communion, and the visible testimonies of God's faithful deliverance throughout history. Prayer becomes a channel through which courage flows, not as mere human bravado, but as a holy boldness forged by intimate knowledge of God's character and promises. It is here that the believer finds the strength to confront spiritual adversaries who seek to sow doubt, division, or despair. Echoing the apostles' exhortation to be watchful and alert in prayer, believers are encouraged to maintain vigilance, recognizing that the struggle is both pervasive and relentless. The prayer of spiritual warfare then becomes a watchtower, a steadfast bulwark holding back the advancing shadows where faith becomes both sword and shield.

Importantly, the nature of spiritual warfare prayer transcends the simplistic clash of good versus evil, presenting a deeply nuanced engagement that involves discernment, humility, and submission. The believers' prayers are permeated by the recognition that they do not fight alone but are participants in a divine drama orchestrated by God. This spiritual reality demands a posture of surrender even while contending, weaving together the paradox of strength in weakness. The model prayer taught by Jesus — the Lord's Prayer — embodies this paradox, petitioning for deliverance from evil while simultaneously affirming the overarching reign of God's kingdom and will. Hence, the prayers of spiritual warfare are suffused with hope and expectancy rather than fear or resignation, reflecting an abiding certainty that divine justice ultimately prevails.

Engaging in spiritual warfare prayer also calls believers to intercede not only for themselves but for others — a communal and expansive dimension where the spiritual well-being of the body of Christ and even the broader creation is encompassed. The apostle Paul's prayers for the churches reveal this expansive intercession, beseeching God's protection against the powers of darkness that threaten unity, faithfulness, and spiritual growth. This intercessory aspect enriches spiritual warfare prayer, transforming it from a personal shield into a communal fortress, where the earnest prayers of many reinforce the strength and resolve of the whole. Such prayers invoke God's peace, protection, and power over every realm of influence that opposes God's will, recognizing that spiritual battles are often fought not in isolation but amidst the intertwined destinies of many believers.

The scriptural narratives also emphasize the importance of aligning spiritual warfare prayers with the revealed will of God, ensuring that such prayers do not slip into impulsive or self-centered petitions but remain grounded in divine truth and righteousness. The prayers of Solomon after the temple's dedication, reflecting an appeal for God's attentive presence in times of conflict, illustrate this alignment — asking not for the removal of all challenges but for the assurance that God's ear is inclined to the prayer of the faithful during trial and lament. This biblical insight challenges believers to cultivate a prayer life that is as much about submission and listening as it is about speaking boldly against spiritual forces. In this way, spiritual warfare prayer becomes an embodied dance of faith — a rhythm of bold petitions, quiet listening, and obedient surrender that unfolds over a lifetime.

Furthermore, the practice of spiritual warfare prayer is inseparable from the fruit of the Spirit, notably love, peace, patience, and self-control. The spiritual combatant's heart must be cultivated in these virtues if the prayers are to reflect God's character rather than human strife. Bitterness, anger, or vengefulness dull the effectiveness of prayer, whereas a loving and humble spirit invites God's intervention and abides under divine protection. Consequently, the biblical images of prayer warriors stand not only as conquerors but as servants — those who enter the fray not out of spite or domination but out of love for God and neighbor. They represent the profound truth that spiritual warfare is ultimately about restoring relationships, healing divisions, and advancing God's peace in a fractured world.

Practically, engaging in spiritual warfare prayer begins with the intentional creation of sacred space — moments carved out from the ceaseless noise and distractions of daily life where the believer can stand firm in the presence of God. Just as Joshua stood firm in battle when the Lord raised his hands, so too believers are called to fix their gaze heavenward, lifting their prayers with deliberate focus and resolve. These prayers incorporate elements of praise that remind of God's power, petitions for divine protection against visible and invisible enemies, and declarations of faith that confront the lies and deceptions wielded by dark forces. They are not confined to formulaic recitations but flow from the well of authentic desperation and hope that characterizes all heartfelt prayer. Methods such as praying scripture back to God, reciting Psalms of protection, or meditating on God's promises fortify the believer's resolve and mirror the biblical tradition of praising God amidst conflict.

The history of the church shows countless testimonies where persistent spiritual warfare prayer opened portals of breakthrough, healing, and deliverance. From early martyrs holding fast in prayer to revival movements ignited by fervent supplication, the spiritual legacy underscores prayer's transformative power in the battleground of faith. Such examples inspire contemporary believers to persevere when confronted with overwhelming odds, cultivating an enduring confidence that prayer changes spiritual realities. This confidence is rooted not in the believer's own power but in Christ's victory over all principalities and powers. When believers pray boldly, they participate in this victory, enacting the reality of Christ's reign in their own lives and communities.

Nevertheless, engaging in spiritual warfare prayer also means embracing moments of vulnerability. There are times when doubt, fatigue, or spiritual desolation may threaten to quench the fire of prayer. The biblical narratives do not ignore these moments; instead, they honor them with stories of saints who wrestled with silence and unanswered prayers, only to emerge strengthened by God's enduring faithfulness. Job's unflinching trust despite his profound suffering, or Jesus' anguished prayers in Gethsemane, reveal that spiritual warfare prayer is not about perfection but persistence. These testimonies reassure believers that even when words fail or prayers seem unanswered, the divine presence remains a steadfast refuge and source of strength. The perseverance in prayer amid spiritual conflict deepens faith, refines character, and invites a deeper union with God's heart.

Ultimately, spiritual warfare prayer is a living conversation — a sacred dialogue that shapes and reshapes the believer's soul, calling forth trust, courage, humility, and love. It rejects passivity in the face of spiritual opposition and instead calls for a vigorous, faithful engagement that acknowledges the gravity of the spiritual realm and the invincible grace of God. Every earnest prayer sent heavenward becomes a whisper to heaven that carries the weight of hope and the promise of victory. In this profound engagement, believers discover that prayer is far more than words; it is a transformative encounter with divine power, a sanctuary in the storm, and a beacon of light overcoming the darkness. As such, to pray boldly and faithfully in spiritual warfare is to embody the promise that no darkness, no force, no trial can ultimately eclipse the radiant dawn of God's redeeming love.

Prayers of Dedication and Commitment

The Meaning of Dedication in Prayer

The meaning of dedication in prayer is a profound and transformative concept, deeply rooted in the essence of human relationship with the divine. It is not merely an act of spoken words or ritualistic repetition, but a solemn covenant—a deliberate and heartfelt commitment—that defines the very posture of the soul. To dedicate oneself in prayer is to enter into a sacred dialogue wherein the supplicant opens not only their lips but also their inner being, offering a pledge of fidelity and faithfulness to God's unfolding plan. This dimension of prayer transcends casual communication; it embodies devotion so complete that it reshapes identity and purpose. In moments of dedication, prayer becomes a crucible where the complexities of human will and divine intention converge, forging a path of alignment that is as challenging as it is ennobling.

Within the biblical narrative, dedication in prayer emerges as both a theme and a call to action, revealing how God's people understand and express their commitment. Throughout scripture, we witness individuals and communities pledging themselves anew to the covenantal relationship with God, often in moments of renewed awakening or critical juncture. These prayers, rich with resolve and submission, show that true dedication involves a surrender of self-will and a heartfelt embracing of divine sovereignty. It is through such profound prayers that characters like Solomon, Hannah, and the early Israelites demonstrate how prayer can serve as a sacred promise, binding their lives with the rhythm of God's purposes. Solomon's prayer at the dedication of the temple stands out vividly as a model of this sanctified commitment, woven with recognition that dedication is not merely a one-time act but an ongoing spiritual reality that demands integrity, humility, and perseverance.

In dedicating oneself through prayer, there is an invitation to encounter God not as a distant observer but as a living presence with whom one consciously chooses to walk in unwavering trust. This trust does not preclude hardship or dissenting emotions but rather welcomes them within the fold of a deeper covenant. The biblical prayers that covenant with God often reveal the tension between human frailty and divine steadfastness—a tension that dedication seeks to resolve by anchoring the heart in divine promises. Whether amid the joyful acknowledgment of God's blessings or the anguished cries for mercy, dedicated prayer creates a sacred space where the individual acknowledges God's authority and aligns their own desires accordingly. This act of alignment is, in many ways, the essence of spiritual maturity, where prayer ceases to be a mere asking and becomes an act of profound surrender and conscious obedience.

Moreover, dedication to prayer carries a transformative power that reorients the believer's entire life trajectory. It is not enough, according to the biblical model, simply to voice commitment; one must live it in concrete acts of faithfulness and love. This is evident in the prayers of Hannah, whose dedication was both a vow and a lived reality as she entrusted her son Samuel to the service of the Lord. Her prayer reflects a dedication that is sacrificial and enduring, illustrating that to dedicate oneself is to offer up not just words but the very core of one's existence. Such dedication becomes a touchstone of identity—a continual realignment with God's purpose that infuses everyday life with holy intention. In this way, prayer as dedication serves both as an inward spiritual compass and as an outward expression of allegiance, embodying a dynamic interplay between divine calling and human response.

The emotional depth and sincerity inherent in dedication prayers underscore the authenticity that true commitment demands. It is not a hollow or perfunctory exercise but one marked by vulnerability and passion. Such prayers often arise out of pivotal life moments—transitions, crises, celebrations—where the speaker realizes the need to reaffirm their dedication to God's guidance and grace. This recognition fuels a prayer that is both a confession of dependence and a declaration of purpose. The notable presence of covenantal language in these prayers—words of binding, consecration, and promise—reflects an ancient understanding that dedication creates an irrevocable bond, a spiritual contract that shapes both present conduct and future hope. The resonance of these prayers endures because they articulate a fundamental human yearning: to live not as aimless wanderers but as devoted children, woven into the fabric of divine love and mission.

Furthermore, dedication as expressed in prayer is inherently relational, calling for an ongoing conversation grounded in faithfulness rather than a one-dimensional pledge. It invites the believer into a lifelong dialogue, a rhythmic back-and-forth where commitment is continuously renewed and deepened. The dedication of the temple by Solomon, followed by his prayer, not only consecrated a physical space but symbolized the covenantal heart of a nation bound to God. This event exemplifies how dedication in prayer encompasses both reverence and responsibility, inspiring worshipers to live in a manner worthy of the sacred trust placed upon them. It shows that dedication is not static but an evolving process—one that nurtures spiritual resilience and cultivates a persistent awareness of God's presence amid the unfolding story of life.

In examining these biblical examples, it becomes evident that dedication invites a holistic transformation, one that infiltrates every facet of existence—thoughts, emotions, choices, and actions—subjugating them to divine will. It is a radical surrender that contrasts sharply with fleeting religious observances. This dedication bridges heaven and earth through the humble act of prayer, turning the intangible whispers of the soul into a covenantal declaration that activates divine partnership. The Psalms, in particular, echo this paradigm with their cycles of lament, praise, and resolve, teaching readers that dedication is often forged through struggle and renewal. Such prayers call forth the courage to persist in faith when circumstances bewilder, reaffirming that dedication is as much about endurance as it is about initial intent.

Transitioning this ancient wisdom to contemporary practice, dedication in prayer remains a vital spiritual discipline for believers seeking authenticity and depth in their communion with God. It challenges modern Christians to move beyond superficial or transactional understandings of prayer and embrace an intentional commitment that requires honesty, patience, and humility. This dedication resists the distractions and noise of a busy world, drawing the believer into a sacred stillness where divine purpose can be discerned with greater clarity. Personal prayer life, enriched by a dedicated posture, becomes a crucible for spiritual growth, offering a sanctuary in which to realign with God's heart and recalibrate life's direction. In doing so, it nurtures a transformative intimacy that informs not only moments of prayer but shapes the entire trajectory of faith and action.

This understanding of dedication also emphasizes the communal dimension of prayer commitment. The biblical prayers that covenant with God were often uttered with or on behalf of others—the community of believers, the nation of Israel, or the household of faith. Dedication, therefore, is not solely a private experience but a collective covenant that binds the faithful together in common purpose and mutual accountability. It encourages believers to hold one another in prayer, fostering solidarity and shared resolve to pursue God's kingdom. This communal aspect reinforces the sacrificial nature of dedication, inviting individuals to transcend self-interest and embrace a vision of collective holiness and mission. Through this, prayer as dedication becomes a powerful instrument of unity and spiritual empowerment.

At its core, the meaning of dedication in prayer is about consecration—not merely setting apart the self but consecrating every thought, decision, and aspiration to the divine will. It is a declarative act that both honors God's sovereignty and acknowledges human dependence, creating a sacred space where divine grace and human resolve coalesce. This sanctified commitment transforms prayer from passive reflection into active engagement, where believers participate in the unfolding divine narrative with intentionality and hope. Just as biblical figures petitioned God with solemn vows, contemporary believers are invited to undertake the same journey of dedication—cultivating prayers that express allegiance, trust, and surrender amid the realities of everyday life.

In practice, this means that dedication in prayer demands careful cultivation of the heart's intentions. It calls for moments of quiet reflection that precede the spoken or silent words, enabling the individual to confront honestly their willingness to commit fully to the divine will. This preparatory stillness fosters a prayerful atmosphere where the soul can be attuned to God's voice, discerning the nuances of divine guidance and purpose. Dedication, then, is a reciprocating movement—a listening as much as a speaking—that deepens spiritual communion and encourages a faithful response. When prayer embodies dedication, it becomes a living testament to God's transforming power and the believer's readiness to embody divine love and justice in the world.

In sum, the meaning of dedication in prayer unfolds as a sacred covenant forged through intentional, heartfelt communication with God. It transcends ritual formality, demanding an authentic, ongoing realignment with divine purpose that encompasses every dimension of life and faith. This dedication is marked by emotional honesty, spiritual resilience, communal solidarity, and transformative surrender. As such, it invites believers into a profound spiritual journey where prayer serves as both expression and enactment of covenantal fidelity. Embracing this view of dedication enriches the prayer experience, making it a dynamic and life-giving relationship that whispers to heaven with sincerity, depth, and unwavering commitment.

Biblical Examples of Dedication

In the vast tapestry of Scripture, moments of dedication burst forth as luminous beacons, each one a sacred covenant between humanity and the Divine, drawing the fragile threads of mortal intention into the grand, eternal design of God's purpose. These biblical examples of dedication illuminate the profound spiritual commitment that prayer can embody—prayers not merely uttered in hurried routines, but solemn vows that weave the fabric of a life wholly given over to God's will. Among the most striking narratives of such covenantal prayer is the dedication of Solomon's temple, a monumental occasion rich with theological and emotional resonance, which serves as an archetype of what it means to consecrate a sacred space and dedicate the heartbeat of a community to the Almighty. Yet, Solomon's prayer of dedication is not merely a historical artifact or an architectural milestone; it is a living testament to the power of communion that embraces every facet of existence—home, heart, and hope intertwined within divine presence.

The story of Solomon's temple dedication unfolds at the very axis of Israel's collective spiritual journey, an epochal event marking the transition from wandering nomads to a settled kingdom grounded in the divine promise. Solomon, the son of David and revered as the wisest ruler of Israel, undertook the construction of the temple as a permanent dwelling place for the Ark of the Covenant, a tangible symbol of God's presence among His people. After years of painstaking labor and unwavering commitment, the temple stood complete, its walls shimmering with gold and precious stones, a physical manifestation of Israel's devotion and God's established covenant. Yet, it is in the prayer Solomon offers at the inauguration of this holy edifice where the spiritual heart of dedication beats most vividly. Solomon's prayer is a sweeping, poetic meditation on God's faithfulness and mercy, expressed in a language that shatters the boundary between the earthly and the divine, inviting all who hear it into an intimate sacred dialogue.

Solomon's words reveal an acute awareness of the delicate tension between human frailty and divine grace. He reminds God and the assembled people that no man, however righteous, can stand in God's presence except through mercy and forgiveness. This serum of humility infused in his prayer defies any notion of arrogance or entitlement; instead, it portrays dedication as a posture of vulnerability and openness. Solomon beseeches God to hear the prayers offered toward the temple—from the prayers of those who seek help in times of distress to the silent longings of those whose hearts are weighed down by sin. His petition is expansive, encompassing not only Israel but all peoples who direct their hearts heavenward, illuminating the temple not merely as a geographical locus but as a spiritual beacon where heaven touches earth. This vision of prayer moves beyond transactional appeals, becoming a covenantal act that aligns human longing with divine compassion, inviting those who call upon the temple to embrace accountability, transformation, and grace.

The grandeur of Solomon's dedication prayer also leaves room for the real, raw messiness of human existence, an honesty that resonates deeply with the Reader today. He acknowledges the inevitability of failure, the times when Israel will sin and "turn away from your commandments." Yet instead of condemning his people, Solomon makes the temple a place for repentance, a sanctuary where forgiveness can be sought and received. This deeply relational understanding of dedication challenges the notion that prayer and commitment are about perfection. Rather, it pictures dedication as an ongoing, dynamic relationship—one that invites confession and renewal as integral parts of a life set apart for God. It asserts that dedication rooted in divine promises creates a space not only for joy and celebration but also for lament and humble return. In this, the temple service yields a rhythm that reflects the human spiritual journey itself, encouraging believers to bring their full selves—their triumphs, sorrows, hopes, and failures—into the sacred dialogue.

Solomon's prayer also underscores the communal nature of dedication, reminding us that devotion is not a solitary endeavor but a shared pilgrimage. The temple served as an anchor for all Israel, embodying the nation's collective identity and spiritual aspirations. The prayer extends an invitation to all present—and to future generations—to join in this covenantal relationship, cultivating a culture of prayer that shaped not just individuals but an entire society. It prompts reflection about how dedication expressed in prayer can ripple through families, communities, and the wider world, binding them into a tapestry of faithfulness and purpose. This collective dimension of devotion moves the act of dedication beyond personal piety to a framework of unity and shared responsibility, reflecting the biblical vision of God's people as a holy and interconnected body. Solomon's prayer becomes a model for communal prayer life, demonstrating how heartfelt dedication contributes to the formation of a resilient spiritual identity, a beacon steadfast amidst the storms of history.

While Solomon's temple dedication prayer stands as a monumental testament to consecration, the Scriptures abound with other poignant examples of dedication that enrich and deepen our understanding of covenantal prayer. The story of Hannah, found in the early chapters of First Samuel, offers a counterpoint that is equally powerful and intimate. Hannah's journey is marked by her fervent longing for a child and the vow she pledges to God if her prayers are answered. In her anguish, Hannah lays bare her soul in raw and aching prayer, a meditation of the heart that moves beyond mere request to a vow of total dedication. Her prayer, filled with emotion and resolve, culminates in a profound act of surrender as she promises to dedicate her son to the Lord's service for his entire life. The birth of Samuel becomes a living symbol of her faithfulness, embodying the profound intersection of human longing and divine action.

Hannah's dedication transcends the simplicity of a promise; it is a sacrificial covenant that shapes the destiny of her child and God's people. In choosing to give Samuel to the Lord's care, she redraws the boundaries of personal desire and spiritual obedience, highlighting the transformative power of prayer as a covenantal act that aligns one's life—and the lives intertwined with it—with divine purpose. Her prayer and vow echo through the ages as a reminder that dedication often involves surrendering what is most precious, trusting wholly in God's providence. This story invites readers to contemplate their own acts of devotion and the layers of meaning attached to the ways they dedicate their gifts, time, and being to God's work.

Moses' prayers, particularly within the wilderness narrative, offer further insight into dedication expressed not only through vows but also through perseverance and intercession. Moses stands repeatedly as the mediator between God and a restless people, and through his prayers, dedication emerges as both a personal commitment and a relentless advocacy for the covenant community. When the Israelites rebel or face hardship, Moses intercedes with a heart burdened for their restoration, offering prayers that are both passionate and persistent. Such prayers illustrate that dedication to God's purposes encompasses enduring faith through struggle, an unyielding pursuit of divine favor, and a resolute commitment to uphold the sacred relationship despite human failings. More than mere ritual, Moses' prayers function as sacred acts of stewardship, entrusted with the well-being of a nation and the faithfulness of the covenant itself.

In the New Testament, the figure of Mary, mother of Jesus, offers a subtle yet profoundly moving glimpse of dedication that intertwines acceptance, trust, and surrender. Her response to the angel Gabriel—"Let it be to me according to your word"—enfolds her entire being in a prayer of radical dedication. This moment reflects an openness to divine will that transcends human understanding, revealing prayer as a profound posture of alignment rather than control. Mary's prayer is a whispered covenant to embrace a path wrought with unknowns, pain, and glory, and her example beckons readers to embrace dedication not only in moments of grand spectacle but in the quiet, persisting "yes" that shapes every day. Her prayer invites reflection on what it means to dedicate one's life to God's plan, an act suffused with trust as much as faithfulness.

Throughout these examples, dedication emerges as multifaceted—as vows, prayers of consecration, continuous acts of intercession, and invitations to surrender personal will for divine purpose. Each narrative reveals that dedication is not a single moment or gesture but a living commitment, unfolding in prayer that breathes life into seemingly ordinary moments and transforms them into dialogues with God. These biblical expressions challenge contemporary readers to see their own prayers not as isolated utterances but as threads woven into the great covenant that spans generations. Dedication, through the lens of Scripture, thus invites a transformational approach to prayer—one that embraces vulnerability, communal identity, and the sacred tension between human yearning and divine sovereignty.

It is also essential to reflect on the sacred spaces these acts of dedication create or sanctify. Solomon's temple, Hannah's home where Samuel grows, the wilderness where Moses intercedes, and the humble setting of Mary's acceptance form tangible contexts where prayer, dedication, and divine encounter converge. These settings remind us that dedication in prayer consecrates not only buildings or moments but the spaces within and around us—our hearts, our homes, and our daily lives. Such consecration heralds a holy rhythm, an invitation to bring ordinary existence into alignment with the sacred, to transform the mundane into an altar of devotion. This perspective urges modern readers to cultivate spiritual environments—both internal and external—that nurture ongoing dedication and open the channels for divine whisperings.

The emotional breadth of these prayers of dedication also offers profound encouragement. They are saturated with hope, fear, joy, sorrow, and trust, depicting prayer as the arena where the fullness of the human spirit meets the vast expanse of God's grace. The dedication prayers exemplify how speaking to God in moments of committing one's life or a sacred space intertwines earnest expectation with humble dependence. This intersection creates a sacred vulnerability that invites God's transformative presence, revealing dedication not as an act of self-sufficiency but as an embrace of divine partnership. Encouraging readers to inhabit this posture means nurturing an attitude of open-hearted prayer, one that honors both the mystery and the intimacy of the relationship with God.

In this light, the biblical examples of dedication communicate a timeless truth: that prayer is a covenantal dialogue where faithful human voices echo through the chambers of eternity, binding lives in sacred promise and divine love. The act of dedication in prayer is thus far more than ritual formality; it is a profound commitment that aligns our deepest desires and actions with God's eternal purpose, shaping destinies and sanctifying moments. This sacred alignment invites a lifelong journey of devotion, beckoning readers to cultivate faithfulness that endures beyond fleeting emotions or circumstances.

Therefore, as one contemplates Solomon's temple dedication and other biblical variants, the heart is drawn into a deeper reflection on how to live a life consecrated in prayer. Like Solomon and Hannah, Moses and Mary, we are called to intertwine our whispers with the divine will, offering prayers that covenant us anew with God. These prayers, born of hope and humility, shape and sustain a spiritual legacy, a melody of dedication that drifts heavenward and echoes back in grace. They ask of us not only the words of prayer but the posture of a heart fully entrusted—a sacred invitation to live and pray with devotion, aligning our lives with a purpose transcending time and place. The biblical narratives affirm that within the embrace of dedication, prayer becomes a sacred dialogue where human vulnerability meets divine faithfulness, and where, in this meeting, our lives find their ultimate meaning and peace.

Committing to God Today

In the quiet depths of every heart, there lies a yearning to belong wholly and without reservation—a sacred desire to be tethered to something eternal and unfailing. The act of committing oneself to God today is not merely a ritual or a fleeting resolution; it is a profound venture into the covenant of the soul, where divine purpose and human devotion entwine in a dance as old as creation itself. As we consider the ancient prayers recorded in scripture, we find numerous voices echoing a profound commitment to the Almighty, voices that bridge the chasm of millennia to speak into our modern lives with fresh urgency and tenderness. To commit to God is to enter a relationship marked by fidelity, surrender, and an intimate alignment with the will of the Divine, thereby transforming the mundane into the sacramental and the fragmented self into a vessel of holy purpose. This commitment is not forged in perfection but in authenticity—acknowledging human frailty while reaching beyond it towards the divine embrace.

The biblical narrative offers a rich tapestry of figures whose prayers reveal the multifaceted textures of spiritual dedication. Consider Hannah, whose heart ached deeply for a child, yet whose supplication transcended personal desire, culminating in a vow that would echo through her life. Her prayer was not simply about an immediate answer; it was imbued with an ongoing pledge to dedicate the child back to the Lord's service, a testament to her willingness to live a life consecrated to God's greater purposes. In her unyielding vulnerability and trust, Hannah models the beauty of commitment that is both tender and resolute—a soul willing to hold dear what is beloved yet release it fully into divine hands. This tension between holding and surrendering is the heartbeat of commitment: a continuous laying down of self-will in favor of divine guidance.

David too, the man after God's own heart, offers a poignant reflection of spiritual devotion. His prayers, cataloged throughout the Psalms, embody a nuanced relationship: one that embraces the full spectrum of human experience—joy, despair, longing, confession, and praise—yet remains anchored in a steadfast allegiance to God. His commitment was not abstract; it was raw and real, marked by moments of failure and redemption, fear and reassurance. The intimacy of David's prayers shows us that commitment is not a static state but an evolving reality, shaped and sharpened by trials and triumphs alike. It is in David's oscillation between frailty and faith that we glimpse the dynamic nature of devotion: it is a living, breathing covenant that deepens when tested, a fire fanned by both reverence and transparency.

To commit to God today means to embrace this dynamic covenant, allowing the words and prayers of these biblical figures to penetrate the routine of daily life and infuse it with sacred intention. Commitment is not an event sealed once and for all but a moment-by-moment yielding to the divine presence that continually calls us back to alignment with our deepest purpose. It is in the small acts of faithfulness—choosing integrity when compromise beckons, extending forgiveness when bitterness tempts, adopting humility when pride surges—that our spiritual dedication takes root and flourishes. These are the whispers of heaven we send forth daily, echoes carried on the winds of our lives as testimonies to our covenantal love.

Yet, commitment to God is more than adherence to duty or moral obligation; it is an invitation into transformation. The prayers of Solomon, for instance, reveal a heart keenly aware of human limitation and divine wisdom. His petition for discernment to govern the people justly reveals a commitment not merely to personal gain but to embodying righteousness on behalf of others. Solomon's prayer exemplifies how sincere dedication demands surrendering our desires for control and embracing God's guidance in shaping our actions. In this surrender, commitment becomes an altar where human aspiration meets divine purpose, and it is here that true spiritual life takes root. It propels believers beyond passive observance to active participation in God's redemptive work in the world.

The challenge of committing to God in contemporary life is profound yet profoundly renewing. Our world, brimming with distractions and incessant noise, often obscures the tender beckoning of the Spirit, urging us back to the sacred ground beneath our restless feet. Yet, in these very moments—amid the chaos, doubt, and brokenness—lies the opportunity to renew our covenantal prayers, to recommit our hearts with fresh sincerity. The act of devotion today means carving out intentional spaces of stillness to listen deeply, to offer prayers that reflect our true longing for divine intimacy and guidance. It involves honest confrontation with the shadowed parts of ourselves that resist surrender, and yet choosing to press forward into the light. The biblical prayers of covenant inspire us to bring both our struggles and our hopes into the holy dialogue with God, knowing that our whispered promises are met with an embrace far greater than we can comprehend.

Mary, the humble servant, embodies the essence of total commitment in her willing "fiat"—her willing "let it be" to God's mysterious plan. Her prayer of submission invites us into a posture of openness where faith and obedience coalesce, where human will finds peace not in dominance but in divine partnership. Mary's example challenges modern believers to relinquish the illusion of control and repose fully in the tender sovereignty of God. This relinquishment is not a loss but a gain in spiritual richness, a deepening of trust that enables us to face uncertainty with courage and hope. Commitment to God today, then, is a daily dance of surrender and trust, an evolving relationship that continuously invites us to choose the path of faith amid the unknown.

As we weave these biblical insights into our own life stories, commitment to God summons us to a kind of spiritual courage that defies easy answers and embraces mystery. It is a holy pursuit that calls for perseverance and grace, a resolve to remain faithful even when prayers seem unanswered or when the divine presence feels distant. This covenantal journey transforms prayer from a transactional exchange into a sacred partnership, where human vulnerability meets divine faithfulness. Each heartfelt pause, each whispered plea, each word of praise becomes part of a mosaic reflecting the sacred covenant that binds us to God. The intentionality of this commitment cultivates resilience, deepens humility, and enriches our spiritual identity.

To live a dedicated spiritual life as exemplified through these biblical prayers is to recognize that commitment is inseparable from relationship. It is not a solitary endeavor but a communion marked by mutual seeking and steadfast love. It summons us to mirror God's unwavering devotion through kindness, justice, and compassion within the world around us. Our prayers, then, become more than words; they become living acts of covenantal engagement, ways to align our daily footsteps with the divine rhythm that orchestrates creation. As we integrate this commitment into every fiber of our being, prayer transforms into a sacred dialogue—a whispered conversation that shapes and steadies us through every season of life.

In choosing to commit ourselves to God today, we are invited into a spiritual narrative where grace and responsibility intertwine. It is a poignant dance where the soul offers its deepest longings and fears, and God responds not with judgment but with steadfast love. This partnership draws us into the light of divine presence, helping us to navigate life's complexities with hope and purpose. The echoes of those ancient prayers grow louder within us, urging a courage that is gentle yet unyielding, a faith that is open yet grounded.

Therefore, the call to commit to God is an invitation not only to speak prayers of devotion but to embody them wholly in the texture of daily living. It calls us to be faithful stewards of our lives, channels of divine light and love, and witnesses to the transformative power of sacred dedication. The covenant forged in the quiet of the heart echoes across generations, binding us to a timeless spiritual lineage as we whisper our own sacred vows to heaven. In embracing this commitment, we begin to live not by mere chance but by divine purpose, our lives radiant with the sacred fire of true devotion.

Prayers of Praise and Thanksgiving Combined

Interconnection of Praise and Thanksgiving

Prayer in its many forms serves as the lifeblood of spiritual communication, a melody woven through the fabric of human experience, carried heavenward on wings of both humility and hope. Among the most intimate and tender threads of this sacred dance are praise and thanksgiving, often intertwined in a seamless embrace that reveals the profound interconnection of adoration and gratitude. When these two prayers merge, they unveil a theological richness that transcends mere ritual or routine, elevating the heart's voice into a vibrant, living dialogue with the Divine. To speak of the interconnection of praise and thanksgiving is to embark on a reflective journey into the very nature of God and the transformative power of acknowledging both who God is and what He graciously gives.

At the heart of praise lies a recognition of God's intrinsic glory and majesty. It is a form of prayer that leaps beyond circumstance, a vaulted exclamation of awe that celebrates the infinite attributes of God—His holiness, sovereignty, justice, mercy, and unchanging faithfulness. Praise is not circumstantial; it does not merely respond to blessings received, nor is it contingent upon life's fortunes. Rather, it is an affirmation of the essence of God in all seasons, expressed in worship that extols the divine character without hesitation or limit. In the biblical narrative, praise resounds like an eternal anthem, from the celestial choir around the throne of God to the impassioned psalms penned by David and the declarations of the prophets. Such praise is foundational: it anchors the believer's identity in the grandeur of God's being, reaffirming a relationship grounded in reverence and joyful surrender.

Thanksgiving, on the other hand, arises from the soil of gratitude. It is the heart's thankful response to God's tangible blessings, both spiritual and material, an acknowledgment of grace received and care bestowed. Thanksgiving is deeply personal; it colors prayers with hues of individual experience and history. The biblical stories are replete with moments of thanksgiving—Hannah's joyful exultation amid longed-for blessing, Solomon's consecration of the temple in grateful recognition of God's faithfulness, and Mary's song of gratitude echoing God's favor upon the humble and powerless. Thanksgiving moves prayer from the abstract realm of divine attributes into the concrete realm of daily life, inviting the believer to recount God's goodness with specificity and warmth.

When praise and thanksgiving unite, the resulting prayer is not a simple summation of two elements but rather a profound synthesis that magnifies the dynamic relationship between God's eternal nature and His present activity in the believer's life. This interconnection forms a cyclical feedback of spiritual awareness: praise for God's unchanging character stirs grateful acknowledgment for blessings bestowed, and thanksgiving for God's benevolence deepens the sense of awe expressed through praise. Together, they create a rich texture of adoration that honors God while embracing the tangible realities of divine grace, generating a holistic spiritual posture of worshipful dependence and joyful recognition.

Theologically, this fusion embodies a truth central to biblical faith— the inseparability of God's being and action. God is not merely an abstract ideal or distant force but a personal, living presence who reveals Himself in both His eternal essence and in compassionate involvement with His creation. The Psalms offer a vivid illustration of this interplay; many psalms begin in praise, marveling at God's sovereignty and holiness, and then move into thanksgiving, recounting specific acts of deliverance and provision. Psalm 100, for instance, beckons all the earth to "Make a joyful noise to the Lord," to serve Him "with gladness," and to "come into His presence with singing," culminating in the exhortation to "Enter his gates with thanksgiving, and his courts with praise!"

This movement within a single psalm from thanksgiving to praise, or vice versa, exemplifies how the biblical text itself weaves these elements together, reflecting the integrated nature of worship.

Moreover, the combination of praise and thanksgiving in prayer nurtures a spiritual posture that is both vertical and horizontal—vertical in its direct adoration toward God's transcendence, and horizontal in its relational acknowledgment of God's interaction within the temporal world. This dual orientation fosters a deeper spirituality, one that does not allow worship to be detached from life's realities nor gratitude to be disconnected from the holiness of God. When believers praise, they express their recognition that God is exalted above all; when they give thanks, they affirm that God's exaltation is made manifest through His provisions and mercies toward humanity. The intertwining of these prayers becomes, therefore, an active stance of faith that embraces both the mystery of God's grandeur and the intimacy of His love.

Another dimension worthy of reflection is how this unity between praise and thanksgiving fosters a transformative rhythm in the believer's soul. Praise often demands a posture of surrender and wonder, opening the heart's gates wide to receive the truth of God's majesty. Thanksgiving, by contrast, requires the contemplative recall of blessings and mercies, an inward turning to count the realities of God's kindness. When these prayers merge, they create a spiritual movement where humility and joy dance together—the worshipper both bows before the infinite God and lifts hands to express heartfelt gratitude for grace mercifully extended. This cyclical motion nourishes spiritual resilience, especially in times of trial, when the act of praising God for His character even amid hardship can prompt thanksgiving for mercies that might easily be overlooked.

Biblical exemplars illuminate this rich interplay vividly. King David, a master of both praise and thanksgiving, embodies this depth in his psalms. His life, marked by fluctuation between triumph and despair, serves as a tableau where praise and thanksgiving are inseparable. In Psalm 34, David extols, "I will bless the Lord at all times; His praise shall continually be in my mouth," followed by a specific recounting of God's deliverance: "Oh, taste and see that the Lord is good!" His prayers artfully combine adoration of God's character with grateful recounting of divine protection. David's example reveals how praise rooted in experiential thanksgiving creates a potent and authentic expression of faith that encompasses both head and heart, doctrine and devotion.

Similarly, Hannah's prayer in 1 Samuel 2 offers a vivid illustration of praise born from thanksgiving. After the long years of barrenness, the gift of a child moves Hannah to sing a song not only of personal gratitude but also of cosmic praise—the lifting up of the lowly, the silencing of the proud, and the acknowledgment of God's sovereign justice. Her prayer transcends a mere litany of thanks; it blossoms into a full-throated hymn of praise, where gratitude and adoration are not separate but converge in a recognition of God's power and mercy. This sacred fusion in prayer points to the holistic engagement of the believer's heart, mind, and spirit.

Reflecting on the nature of praise and thanksgiving also brings to light their indispensability for nurturing a balanced spiritual life. A prayer life rich in praise but devoid of thanksgiving risks becoming abstract, disconnected from the rhythms of lived experience and the tangible evidences of God's grace. Conversely, thanksgiving without praise may slip into being merely transactional or utilitarian—focused on what is received rather than who is received. The blending of these prayers restores equilibrium, ensuring worship is both an acknowledgment of God's eternal grandeur and an affirmation that God actively works in history and personal life. It deepens faith by cultivating an awareness that God's worthiness to be praised is inseparable from His gracious engagement with His people.

The spiritual implications extend further into the communal life of faith. Congregational worship, when permeated by prayers combining praise and thanksgiving, models a collective hospitality of the Spirit, inviting the faith community to participate in this holistic dialogue with God. Such prayers enrich the shared experience of worship, enabling individuals to bring their personal gratitude into the corporate anthem of praise. The blending encourages believers to celebrate both the majestic character of God and the gifts received, fostering unity in diversity, as each person's voice adds a unique note to the chorus of adoration and thanks. In this way, the interconnection of praise and thanksgiving strengthens ecclesial bonds and cultivates a shared spiritual identity centered on recognizing and honoring God's multifaceted presence.

From a practical perspective, embracing the intertwining of praise and thanksgiving invites a particular mindset in prayer life that can deepen spiritual hunger and widen the scope of divine encounter. It urges the believer to cultivate attentiveness—not only to God's magnificence but also to the myriad ways God's goodness is manifest day by day. This spiritual attentiveness transforms prayer into a sacred dialogue where noticing and naming God's works go hand in hand with affirming God's eternal worth. Such intentional prayer nurtures an ongoing awareness that each blessing is not isolated but rooted in the character of a God who is worthy of unwavering praise.

In application, believers might find this fusion reflected in the rhythm of their daily prayer practices, beginning by simply acknowledging God's unchanging nature—His holiness, love, justice, and mercy—lifting up praise as an act of worshipful recognition. This opening often softens the soul, preparing it to engage with thankfulness for specific gifts or moments of grace encountered throughout the day. By allowing praise and thanksgiving to flow into one another naturally, prayer becomes a spiraling ascent where adoration fuels gratitude, and gratitude magnifies adoration. This dynamic interplay becomes a spiritual lifeline, sustaining hope and deepening intimacy with God in the midst of life's ebb and flow.

Moreover, this combined prayer fosters a more authentic encounter with God that embraces the whole human experience. It invites worshippers to bring not only their joys but also their surprises, recognizing that adoration is strengthened when it arises from grateful hearts aware of God's tangible presence. The act of thanking God serves to ground the heavenly aspirations of praise, anchoring worship in life's realities and reinforcing the truth that God's character is not detached from His daily acts of kindness and provision. Consequently, prayer becomes an organic expression, seamless and profoundly real, allowing the believer to live out a faith that honors God's transcendence without neglecting God's immanence.

In essence, the interconnection of praise and thanksgiving reveals prayer as a living, breathing dialogue where God's infinite worthiness and gracious acts are intimately linked. This synthesis invites believers to journey deeper into the mystery of divine-human encounter, where the awe of worship and the warmth of gratitude form a sacred covenant of mutual love. Every whisper of praise enriched by thanksgiving becomes a fragrant offering, a sacred breath rising heavenward—one that recognizes God not only as the eternal King enthroned in glory but also as the faithful lover who showers blessing upon blessing with unwavering compassion. Such prayers resonate through eternity, echoing the timeless truth that acknowledging who God is and giving thanks for what God does are inseparable acts of a heart surrendered wholly to the divine.

Biblical Illustrations

Throughout the tapestry of Scripture, moments emerge where praise and thanksgiving stand not as separate threads but are woven seamlessly together into hymns of heartfelt adoration. These biblical illustrations unveil a profound truth: that recognizing God's sovereign, holy nature naturally stirs the soul to gratitude for His manifold mercies. As one reads through the sacred texts, it becomes clear that praise and thanks are not mere ritualistic utterances but an organic duet of the spirit, reflecting an intimate awareness of who God is alongside a deep appreciation for what He has done. This dynamic interplay between adoration and gratitude invites the reader into a living encounter with the divine, where the heart overflows, compelled both to exalt God's glorious name and to acknowledge the blessings flowing from His hands with thankful reverence.

Consider, for instance, the majestic opening of Psalm 100, where the psalmist calls the people of Israel to "Make a joyful noise to the Lord, all the earth! Serve the Lord with gladness! Come into his presence with singing!" In these verses, praise bursts forth exuberantly, an acknowledgment of God's sovereign rule over all creation — "For the Lord is good; his steadfast love endures forever, and his faithfulness to all generations." Here, the adoration of God's unchanging character flows effortlessly into thanksgiving. The psalmist does not separate the worship of God's nature from grateful recognition of His ongoing faithfulness; rather, he binds them together as essential expressions of a faithful heart. This unity teaches us that true praise is incomplete without the thankful remembrance of God's deeds, just as genuine gratitude is sustained by a conscious regard for God's holy nature.

The narrative of Hannah in 1 Samuel 2 provides another vivid illustration where praise and thanks merge into an inspired song of devotion. Before she bore her promised child, Samuel, Hannah had suffered great anguish over her barrenness, pouring out her soul in prayer to the Lord. When her prayers were answered, her heart leapt not only with thanksgiving but with utter praise to God's unmatched might and justice. In her song, Hannah exalts God's sovereignty: He "raises the poor from the dust" and "keeps the feet of his faithful ones," a recognition of God's character as the righteous judge and merciful provider. At the same time, her thanksgiving for the personal blessing of answered prayer floods her song with joy. There is no sterile separation between honoring God's transcendent nature and blessing Him for His intimate involvement in her life. Instead, Hannah's prayer blooms as a fragrant offering combining both adoration and gratefulness, demonstrating how acknowledgment of God's power inspires a thankful response that acknowledges His tangible presence and grace.

Solomon's prayer at the dedication of the temple stands as another monumental biblical moment where praise harmonizes intimately with thanksgiving. As he lifts his voice to the heavens, Solomon recognizes the incomprehensible glory of the Lord who dwells beyond human reach, declaring, "But will God indeed dwell with man on the earth? Behold, the heavens and the highest heaven cannot contain you, how much less this house that I have built!" This exclamation reflects profound awe for God's infinite greatness, a rightful praise of His transcendence and holiness. Yet the prayer does not stop there—it weaves in solemn thanksgiving for the favor God has shown in permitting His name to be established in the temple, for the answered prayers and abundant blessings the Lord has bestowed. Solomon's prayerscape is thus a tapestry of praise and thanks where adoration for God's majesty naturally pours forth alongside gratefulness for His covenant faithfulness, illustrating how worship becomes richest when it integrates these two dimensions.

In the New Testament, the prayers of Jesus frequently exemplify this same union, particularly in moments of deep intimacy with the Father. The most striking example may be found in the Gospel of Luke during the Last Supper, when Jesus offers thanks before breaking the bread, saying, "Father, I thank you that you have heard me." Here, gratitude flows from the heart of the Son even as He prepares to fulfill the divine will, acknowledging the Father's attentive ear and loving provision. Yet within this act of thanksgiving, there is profound praise embedded in the recognition of God's faithful presence and sovereignty over unfolding events. Jesus' prayer epitomizes a seamless combination of exaltation and gratefulness, reminding us that even in suffering and uncertainty, the bedrock of prayer lies in honoring God's nature while giving thanks for His guiding hand.

The Apostle Paul's letters offer abundant evidence of this intermingling of praise and thanksgiving as well. In his epistles to the churches, Paul frequently begins with doxologies intertwined with expressions of gratitude. For example, in Philippians, he writes, "I thank my God in all my remembrance of you, always in every prayer of mine for you all, making my prayer with joy." Paul's language reveals that his thanksgiving for the believers is inseparable from his praise of God, who works powerfully through their lives. This blending is not an abstract theological idea but a lived experience, displaying how a heart attuned to God's presence overflows both in praising His character and in giving thanks for His active work in the lives of others and himself. Such prayer demonstrates a spiritual vision where praise for God's glory and thanksgiving for His blessings are intertwined strands reflecting a unified voice rising heavenward.

The Book of Revelation, with its apocalyptic imagery and celestial visions, ultimately brings this fusion of praise and thanks to its fullest expression. The multitude gathered before the throne of God ceaselessly proclaims, "Worthy is the Lamb who was slain, to receive power and wealth and wisdom and might and honor and glory and blessing!" At the same time, this worshipful assembly declares thanksgiving to the Lord, for He alone is worthy of praise because of His redemptive work and eternal reign. This eternal chorus moving through the heavenly courts encapsulates the essence of worship where praise for God's inherent worth and thanksgiving for His salvific actions are inseparably joined, presenting a timeless pattern that invites earthly believers into the same adoring gratitude. It is a portrayal of worship as a living breath—both exaltation and appreciation—offered perpetually to the Divine.

In many of the Psalms, the interweaving of praise and thanksgiving forms a thematic heartbeat resonating throughout the entire Psalter. Psalm 103, often called the "Psalm of Praise," impels the soul to "Bless the Lord, O my soul, and all that is within me, bless his holy name!" With eloquence, it acknowledges the Lord's forgiveness, healing, redemption, provision, and steadfast love, extolling both His nature and His acts. The psalmist expresses adoration not merely for God's inherent goodness but expressly thanks Him because those attributes manifest in tangible mercies to the faithful. This dual movement creates a rhythm where praise flows into thanksgiving, and thanksgiving deepens praise, reflecting a spiritual cycle that sustains sincere communion with God. The psalmist shows that it is impossible to separate the declaration of God's greatness from the grateful rejoicing over His benefits, as one nurtures the other and raises the heart heavenward.

Examining the prayers of Moses also reveals this confluence of praise and gratitude. When God leads the Israelites out of Egypt, Moses frequently calls the people to remember, to praise God for His mighty acts, and to give thanks for His providence and guidance. In Exodus, after the parting of the Red Sea, Miriam and the women sang a song of "praise and thanksgiving," extolling God who triumphed over the enemies of His people. This praise, deeply rooted in God's saving power, naturally becomes thanksgiving, underscoring how acknowledging divine deliverance leads the worshiper into a heart overflowing with gratitude. These prayers, often spontaneous and borne out of recognition of God's immediate action, illustrate how praise and thankfulness become inseparable in moments of divine intervention and grace.

David's life is a rich reservoir of prayers that intertwine adoration and gratitude across seasons of triumph and trial. The intensity of his psalms reflects a soul deeply acquainted with God's presence, often erupting into exultant praise for God's righteousness and steadfast love. Yet alongside this, David continually offers thanksgiving for deliverance, protection, and answered pleas. His voice never hesitates to proclaim not only the greatness of God but also to thank Him warmly for His active care. This fusion mirrors the complexity of human experience before the Divine: a recognition of God's exalted nature coupled with heartfelt appreciation for His daily mercies. David's example invites readers to express their own prayers as vibrant, living conversations that honor God's essence and celebrate His blessings without partition.

The unity of praise and thanksgiving in biblical prayers extends beyond individual expression into corporate worship, where communities acknowledge God's grandeur while giving thanks as a collective response to His grace. The Book of Nehemiah, for example, records settings where the Israelites gathered to pray, praising God as King and thanking Him for restoring their fortunes and rebuilding the walls of Jerusalem. These public declarations of both admiration and grateful remembrance reveal an understanding that communal prayer embraces the dual vocation of honoring God's eternal nature and celebrating His tangible involvement in communal life. The blending of praise and thanks here nourishes a collective identity rooted in God's faithfulness, fostering a dynamic spirituality that echoes through generations.

In the New Testament epistle to the Hebrews, we find a theological reflection reinforcing this link between praise and thanksgiving. The author exhorts believers to "offer to God acceptable worship, with reverence and awe"—an offering that is intrinsically linked to gratitude for salvation and the revelation of God in Christ. The act of worship thus becomes impossible to disentangle from thanksgiving; the very gesture of lifting God up in praise is the outcrop of a thankful heart touched by divine grace. This intertwining shapes a powerful spiritual posture toward God, inviting believers to enter into prayer not as a mere form but as a living response of awe-filled thanks that worships the divine character manifested in Christ.

The birth narratives also reflect the harmony of praise and thanksgiving. When Mary, pregnant with Jesus, visits Elizabeth, the Magnificat bursts forth—one of the Bible's most beautiful prayers blending exaltation of God's holiness and mighty deeds with profound gratitude for being chosen as His humble servant. Mary declares, "My soul magnifies the Lord, and my spirit rejoices in God my Savior!" Her prayer is a vibrant expression where praise for God's justice and mercy becomes inseparable from heartfelt thanks for personal blessing and grace. This intimate encounter between divine praise and humble gratitude invites readers to see their own prayers as multifaceted, carrying both reverent adoration and personal thanksgiving in one breath.

In reflecting on these biblical examples, one notes that praise and thanksgiving find their fullest expression when the worshiper recognizes God's inherent worth and character as the source from which blessings flow. Praise, the acknowledgment of God's glory, holiness, and power, does not stand apart from thanksgiving, the heart's response to God's merciful interventions and gifts. The Scriptures teach that adoration often precedes and shapes gratitude, while thankfulness enriches and gives context to praise. Far from being static or formal, this relationship invites a dynamic conversation where the soul, ever aware of God's majesty, responds with a grateful heart for His daily faithfulness. Through these narratives and prayers, the reader is guided toward a richer, more integrated spiritual life—one where praise and thanks are communion partners, leading the believer deeper into the mystery and joy of heartfelt prayer.

As the reader contemplates these united forms of prayer, it may be helpful to imagine the landscape of worship not as a procession of isolated expressions but as a flowing river, where praise and thanksgiving intermingle like waters merging into one stream. This imagery conveys how, in the act of prayer, recognizing God's greatness stirs our spirits to thankfulness, and our gratitude, in turn, nurtures a deeper longing to exalt His name. The biblical illustrations thus provide a living map: by embracing praise and thanks as partners rather than competitors in prayer, we discover a profound unity of devotion, an intimate whisper to heaven that resonates with the joyful acknowledgment of God's glory and the peaceful certainty of His benevolent presence.

In this unified approach to prayer, the believer's voice joins a chorus echoed through millennia—a voice rising with the psalmists, prophets, apostles, and saints who knew well that praising God for who He is cannot be separated from thanking Him for what He does. This realization invites readers not only to study these biblical models but also to embody them in their own prayer lives, cultivating a vibrant spiritual practice where the heart's adoration blossoms naturally into gratitude. As one prays, it becomes clear that praise and thanksgiving are not merely parallel exercises but intertwined pathways guiding us into a richer encounter with God, transforming whispered words into a sacred song that ascends heavenward, echoing the eternal worship of the divine.

Incorporating Combined Prayer

To embrace a holistic understanding of prayer is to open one's heart not merely to isolated expressions of praise or thanksgiving, but to the intertwining of these divine conversations—an interplay where adoration seamlessly flows into gratitude, where recognition of God's transcendent nature kindles a thankful spirit, and where the soul's deepest awe is matched by a humble acknowledgment of blessings received. In the sacred texts of scripture, we witness this dynamic dance repeated with power and beauty: prayer that does not stand as separate fragments of experience, but as a living, breathing whole. Such prayers pulse with a vibrant rhythm—an ever-evolving dialogue that nurtures a fuller and richer communion with God. They invite us to consider prayer not as a checklist of expressions but as an organic outpouring of the heart, an inward journey set aflame by the knowledge of who God is and what He has graciously done.

When we speak of incorporating combined prayer, we are encouraged to break free from the compartmentalized approach that tends to pigeonhole praise in one corner and thanksgiving in another. Instead, a unified tapestry emerges where the two weave inseparably. Imagine the psalmist David, whose words often begin with majestic glorification of the Lord's eternal sovereignty and boundless power and then shift effortlessly into personal recounting of God's mercies, provision, and deliverances. In Psalm 100, for instance, we are invited to "Make a joyful noise to the Lord, all the earth! Serve the Lord with gladness!

Come into His presence with singing! Know that the Lord, He is God! It is He who made us, and we are His; we are His people, and the sheep of His pasture. Enter His gates with thanksgiving, and His courts with praise! Give thanks to Him; bless His name!" These words reveal a sweeping movement from adoration, a recognition of God's intrinsic nature as Creator and Shepherd, into a heartfelt response of gratitude. This fusion creates a totality of worship that can envelop the worshiper's entire being.

To cultivate such prayers is to nurture an awareness that the awe that springs from God's holiness and majesty naturally prepares the soil for gratitude to take root. When we acknowledge God's grandeur—His unchanging character, His boundless wisdom, and His unfailing goodness—we do not do so in isolation. The recognition of who God is never exists without an impact on our hearts as recipients of His grace. Gratitude arises not merely as a polite response but as a profound consequence of truly seeing God's nature. This is an experience of the soul where adoration and thanksgiving fuse, imparting warmth and life to prayer. They are not discrete acts but a spiritual fusion that mirrors the multifaceted relationship God longs to dwell in with us. The sky does not separate the light of the sun from the warmth it brings; so too, prayer's warmth cannot be severed from its light.

This combined prayer finds breathtaking expression in the words of Solomon at the dedication of the temple, where praise and thanksgiving converge into a sweeping proclamation. There, Solomon extols the Lord's faithfulness, His covenantal steadfastness, and His unmatched glory while simultaneously offering thanks for the fulfillment of the long-awaited promise to establish a place where God's name would dwell among His people. His prayer captures the sacred pulse of gratitude borne out of a deep appreciation of God's divine nature and wondrous deeds. When we study such prayers, we realize that this seamless melding of worship is a divine invitation to experience prayer as a dynamic, relational event, absorbing and reflecting the vitality of God's presence.

The psychological and spiritual dimensions of this integrated prayer practice reveal a profound truth about human spiritual experience. Adoration reminds the soul of the infinite vastness of God, creating a space of humility and reverence that frees us from our preoccupations and anxieties. This sense of awe cultivates a mental and emotional landscape where gratitude can flourish. Gratitude then softens the heart, awakening a joyful response to all that flows from God's hands—life, providence, forgiveness, and grace. The two together engage the full spectrum of our being: adoration stirs the intellect and imagination toward God's transcendence, while thanksgiving enlivens the emotions by drawing attention to concrete blessings. When these forces converge, prayer transforms from a mere religious duty to an intimate encounter filled with vitality and depth.

From a practical standpoint, encouraging this blended form of prayer requires sensitivity to the rhythm of one's spiritual life and a willingness to let go of rigid expectations in prayer practice. It invites an openness to listen deeply to the movements of the heart as it responds spontaneously to God's revelation. One might begin with a posture of adoration— reflecting on God's holiness, wisdom, or love—allowing the heart to swell in awe. From this elevated vantage point, the soul naturally transitions into thanksgiving, recounting personal and communal blessings received, from daily mercies to significant moments of divine intervention. This flow is a spiritual dance, a sacred interweaving that enriches the texture of prayer and fosters a fuller awareness of God's nearness. Prayers become textured and alive, flowing in rhythms that resemble the Psalms, which serve as enduring models of this holistic engagement.

Moreover, adopting combined prayer addresses a common spiritual challenge: the fragmentation of prayer life. Often, believers compartmentalize their communication with God—saving praise for worship services, reserving thanksgiving for routine prayers, and relegating supplication or confession to moments of crisis. This segmented approach can inadvertently limit the depth of connection experienced in prayer. By blending adoration and gratitude, believers reclaim the wholeness of prayer as a continuous flow that reflects God's multifaceted presence in all life's dimensions. The spiritual fruits are manifold: enhanced joy, growing trust, a renewed sense of awe, and a cultivated habit of noticing God's workings both in grand miracles and quiet moments. The practice fosters resilience, grounding the soul in a perspective that no matter the circumstance, God's nature invites reverence and His blessings merit gratitude.

This integrated prayer model also carries theological significance, reminding us that God's identity revealed in scripture is inseparable from His activity in history and in our lives. The Psalms, prophetic writings, and the prayers within the New Testament illuminate God as the sovereign Creator, a covenant-keeper, and an intimate presence among His people. When prayer calls attention to both who God is and what He has done, it honors that divine unity. To lift God up in adoration without acknowledging His enduring faithfulness to His promises and His ongoing provision risks becoming an abstract theology devoid of relational warmth. Conversely, offering thanks without a grounding sense of God's sovereign character may reduce gratitude to mere acknowledgment of gifts rather than a worshipful response to divine grace. Hence, in the biblical witness, combined prayer embodies a theology of relationship that calls the believer into a holistic honoring of God's being and deeds.

As readers cultivate this kind of prayer, they may discover that their spiritual perceptions deepen, allowing them to trace the contours of God's presence both in the magnificent and the mundane. Daily life, often cluttered with distractions and challenges, can become a sacred space when approached with a prayerful heart that simultaneously magnifies God's greatness and recognizes His tender mercies. This dual focus shapes a spiritual lens, transforming our worldview and heightening spiritual sensitivity. Practically, it can refine the way individuals journal their prayers, encouraging a reflective style that begins by contemplating God's attributes before moving into recounting blessings. It may also inspire communal worship, where groups are invited to join in prayers that embody this fusion, strengthening collective awareness of God's multifaceted interaction with His people.

The richness of combined prayer also suggests a dynamic spirituality characterized by balance—where neither the abstract nor the concrete dominates but both inform and elevate the other. Adoration without thanksgiving can drift toward theological abstraction, whereas thanksgiving without adoration risks reducing God to a dispenser of blessings. The harmonious blend reveals prayer as a precise yet fluid expression reflecting the fullness of God's nature and human response. This balance mirrors the biblical narrative itself, one that consistently speaks of a God both transcendent and immanent, glorious and gracious, mighty and merciful. Through prayer that blends these elements, believers participate in the divine rhythm of praise and gratitude that has echoed through the ages.

Finally, incorporating combined prayer invites a posture of humility and vulnerability before God. It requires honesty—acknowledging moments when adoration arises with difficulty, or when gratitude feels pressured rather than spontaneous. It invites patience with oneself in the unfolding of authentic prayer life and encourages perseverance in seeking a deeper encounter with God. Embracing this holistic approach means surrendering the desire for formulaic prayers and embracing the mystery of relational dialogue. Prayer becomes not only words spoken or thoughts formulated but a sacred exchange where God's nature stirs the heart and His blessings awaken the spirit, merging into a continuous whisper rising to heaven. In this embrace, prayer transcends its basic function and becomes the very breath of spiritual life, a sacred song that harmonizes adoration and thanksgiving into a melody pleasing to the divine ear.

The Lord's Prayer: Model and Pattern

Structure of the Lord's Prayer

The Lord's Prayer stands as a cornerstone of Christian prayer, a divinely inspired template that weaves together the threads of praise, petition, confession, and commitment into a seamless tapestry of spiritual communication. In its simplicity, it carries profound depths, each phrase unfolding layers of meaning that extend beyond mere words, inviting the heart into devoted alignment with God's will. To truly appreciate this prayer's enduring power, one must delve into its structure, examining each component not as isolated expressions but as integral movements within a sacred dialogue. This exploration reveals the multiplicity of prayer's nature embodied in a compact form, showing how the Lord's Prayer serves as an ever-relevant guide for all who seek to commune honestly and vibrantly with the Divine.

The opening invocation, "Our Father who art in heaven," immediately establishes the relationship and the setting for the conversation. By addressing God as Father, the prayer acknowledges an intimate, familial bond that transcends formality yet commands reverence. The term "Our" expands the personal connection into a communal embrace, reminding the worshipper that prayer is not solely an individual endeavor but a shared expression of faith among the body of believers. Placing God "in heaven" situates Him as sovereign and transcendent, above earthly limitations, inviting awe and recognition of divine majesty. This duality — a loving Father yet exalted sovereign — refines the prayer's entire tone, balancing closeness with respect, warmth with awe. It draws the petitioner into a humble posture, heart attuned to both intimacy and holiness.

Following the address, the prayer moves into a rhythm of praise with the phrase, "Hallowed be thy name." To "hallow" means to make holy, to revere intensely, which here becomes a foundational act of worship within prayer. This petition is both declarative and aspirational: it acknowledges God's inherent holiness and simultaneously calls upon all humanity to honor His name accordingly. The phrase evokes an entire cosmos where God's name—symbolic of His character and presence—is to be treated with the utmost sanctity. It's a moment where the individual's mind is lifted beyond personal concerns toward the recognition of divine glory, helping the prayer rise above routine into the realm of sacred praise. This expression also serves as a spiritual anchor, orienting the heart to God's holiness before venturing into petitions, a practice essential for maintaining reverence amid requests.

Next, the prayer turns toward God's kingdom with the petition, "Thy kingdom come." This phrase carries a weighty theological depth, encapsulating the longing for God's sovereign reign to be fully realized on earth as it is in heaven. Implicit here is the recognition of a present yet incomplete reality—a kingdom inaugurated by Christ's life, death, and resurrection but awaiting consummation in its fullness. By praying for the kingdom's arrival, believers express hope for justice, peace, and the dismantling of evil's hold on the world. It is a prayer that invites a radical transformation not only in cosmic terms but also in the personal heart and community life. Hence, it fuels a spiritual expectancy, inspiring active participation in God's unfolding purposes and a readiness to embody kingdom values here and now.

Closely linked to the coming kingdom is the plea, "Thy will be done on earth as it is in heaven." This petition harmonizes desire for divine sovereignty with submission, emphasizing God's perfect will as the highest aim. It acknowledges human limitation in discerning or fulfilling God's purposes independently and expresses a surrender of one's agenda in favor of divine direction. The phrase contrasts the often disorderly and broken state of earthly existence with the perfect obedience and harmony of heaven, implying a transformative prayer for reality itself to be conformed to God's ideal. In this sense, it is a call for an ongoing inner renewal and outward witness, challenging believers to align their daily lives with God's revealed will, thus becoming channels of heaven's peace and truth amid a fractured world.

Having established a foundation of praise and alignment with God's holiness and purpose, the prayer moves into personal petitions beginning with "Give us this day our daily bread." This request shifts the focus from the cosmic to the practical, embodying dependence on God's providence for sustenance and life's necessities. "Daily bread" symbolizes not only physical nourishment but also a broader category of God's ongoing grace and provision. It confronts human vulnerability head-on, acknowledging that survival and well-being hinge on divine generosity delivered each day anew. The temporal specificity of "this day" imbues the prayer with immediacy and trust in God's faithful care, rejecting anxiety about the future in favor of present reliance. This segment beautifully balances the sacred eternal with the tangible temporal, teaching believers to bring their ordinary, daily needs into the sacred dialogue with God.

The prayer then tenderly introduces the vital theme of forgiveness, both receiving and extending it, with the phrase, "And forgive us our trespasses, as we forgive those who trespass against us." This confession is vital in the prayer's rhythm, for it acknowledges human brokenness and the essential need for mercy. The term "trespasses" signals offenses against God's law and neighbor, embedding the confession within a communal reality of sin and reconciliation. It is a moment of raw vulnerability, where the individual admits personal failings and simultaneously commits to forgiving others, highlighting the reciprocal nature of divine forgiveness and human relationships. This mutual forgiveness is a radical call to mirror God's grace in daily life, transforming hearts and healings wounds within communities. The prayer here cultivates humility, repentance, and a commitment to mercy, essential for maintaining spiritual health and fostering restoration.

Continuing in the realm of spiritual guidance and protection, the prayer petitions, "And lead us not into temptation." This phrase reveals prayer's role as a shield in the ongoing battle with moral and spiritual challenge. The acknowledgment that believers face temptations humanizes the spiritual journey, affirming the reality of internal struggles and external pressures designed to derail faithfulness. To ask God's leading away from temptation is both a surrender of will and a proactive request for divine strength and wisdom to navigate life's pitfalls. Importantly, it presupposes God's role as a guide whose intervention is necessary to preserve a life of integrity and holiness. This phrase encapsulates prayer's protective function, asking for direction and deliverance from forces that threaten spiritual health.

Closely tied to temptation is the plea, "But deliver us from evil." Here, the prayer extends beyond personal sin to encompass the broader realm of evil's destructive power. The term "evil" carries connotations of moral corruption, spiritual oppression, and the pervasive brokenness afflicting the world. Deliverance is a profound appeal for rescue, liberation, and protection from all that opposes God's kingdom and defiles human existence. This plea recognizes the existential reality of evil's presence and power while affirming trust in God's ultimate authority and victory. The prayer transitions here from requests for direction to appeals for salvation, underscoring the believer's need for divine intervention not only in moments of weakness but as a continual spiritual safeguard.

Many versions of the Lord's Prayer conclude with a doxology, "For thine is the kingdom, and the power, and the glory, forever." Though absent in some early manuscripts, this concluding affirmation powerfully summarizes the theological truths the entire prayer hinges. It reasserts the sovereignty and might of God as ultimate realities that encompass and transcend human experience. Declaring God's kingdom, power, and glory as eternal comforts the heart and affirms faith in God's triumph amidst the world's uncertainties. It elevates the prayer's tone from petition to praise once again, creating a cyclical flow that begins and ends in adoration. The doxology reinforces the spiritual orientation established at the beginning, reminding believers that prayer is rooted in the worship of a mighty, everlasting God—one worthy of unwavering devotion and trust.

Taken as a whole, the Lord's Prayer artfully balances the vertical and horizontal dimensions of spirituality. It opens with recognition of God's grandeur and nearness, draws the petitioner into profound submission, intertwines personal needs with communal responsibility, and closes with an assurance of divine sovereignty. It embodies praise by acknowledging God's holiness, kingdom, and power, modeling thanksgiving through trust in providence, fosters confession in its plea for forgiveness, expresses lament in its desire for deliverance from evil, and epitomizes commitment through surrender to God's will and readiness to forgive others. This multifaceted engagement invites believers not into a monotonous routine but a living dialogue, rich with emotional nuance and theological depth.

Moreover, the prayer's structure reflects a holistic spirituality that nurtures the whole person by addressing mind, heart, and will. It stimulates worship in the intellect by affirming divine attributes, engages the affections through honest openness about human frailty and needs, and cultivates the will to obey and forgive. This integration exemplifies how prayer transcends simple communication—becoming a transformational encounter where the soul is shaped and aligned with divine purposes. For contemporary believers, the Lord's Prayer remains a profound resource, its balanced structure providing a framework that adapts fluidly to various contexts—private meditation, corporate worship, or intercessory prayer—offering a timeless language to articulate the deepest longings and loyalties of the spirit.

In reading and praying the Lord's Prayer attentively, one discovers that its power lies not only in words but in the movement it creates within the soul. It opens the heart with reverence, focuses attention on God's grandeur and grace, invites vulnerability through confession, fosters communal empathy through shared petitions, and reinforces faith through trust and commitment. Each phrase acts as a gentle step guiding the pilgrim deeper into the sacred space where human fragility meets divine strength. This dynamic rhythm—between praise and petition, confession and surrender—embodies the full spectrum of prayer's purpose: to draw humanity closer to God, to transform suffering and hope alike, and to forge an enduring bond that whispers continually to heaven.

Theological Significance

In reflecting upon the Lord's Prayer, one cannot merely skim its words as a rote formula; rather, one must delve into the profound theological bedrock upon which it rests, uncovering layers of meaning that resonate through the corridors of Christian faith and practice. This prayer, given by Jesus Himself in the quiet intimacy of the Sermon on the Mount, is pregnant with significance, embodying the multidimensional essence of prayer as both an invocation of divine presence and a human response woven with reverence, need, repentance, and resolve. To approach the Lord's Prayer simply as a model of what to say is to overlook its immense depth as a theological statement—each phrase acts as an axis around which rotate the core concerns of our spiritual existence, speaking to the holiness of God, the nature of His kingdom, the reality of sin, and the ethics of living under His gaze.

Beginning with the opening address, "Our Father in heaven," the prayer immediately situates the believer in a context that is both intimate and awe-inspiring. The divine is not a distant monarch but a loving Father, a personal being who invites us into a familial relationship. Yet, the addition of "in heaven" roots this intimate connection within the transcendent reality of God's sovereignty, reminding us that this Father's love is infused with majesty and holiness beyond the earthly realm. This juxtaposition carries deep theological weight: it unites the immanence of

God with His transcendence, compelling believers to recognize that prayer is the meeting place of human frailty and divine glory. It is a sacred dialogue that acknowledges our dependence while honoring the holiness that sets God apart. Theologically, this opening line challenges simplistic conceptions of God, expanding them into a relationship that balances accessibility with reverence—God is near to us as a Father, yet infinitely exalted above us, a tension that shapes the entire prayer.

The subsequent phrase, "Hallowed be your name," unfolds the theological mystery of God's holiness as a dynamic reality rather than a static attribute. To hallow God's name is to acknowledge and affirm His sanctity, to set apart His character as holy and worthy of worship. It encapsulates the believer's participation in the divine holiness—prayer becomes an act of consecration, an invitation to deepen one's awareness of God's sacredness. In the biblical worldview, a name is not merely a label but the embodiment of one's essence and presence. Thus, to sanctify the name of God is to honor the fullness of who He is—as Creator, Judge, Redeemer, and Sustainer of all things. This phrase serves as a theocentric orientation, reminding the faithful that prayer is not about human desires alone, but about aligning one's heart with the glory and honor of God. It elevates the prayer beyond mere petition, transforming it into an act of worship that sets the divine nature at the center of one's spiritual focus.

When we say, "Your kingdom come, your will be done, on earth as it is in heaven," the prayer enters the realm of eschatological longing and ethical submission. This petition resonates with a profound theological hope: the anticipation of God's sovereign reign fully realized in the present world and in the fullness of time. The kingdom of God is a central motif in Jesus' teaching, representing not only a future reality but also a present spiritual condition—a reign characterized by divine justice, peace, and mercy. Here, prayer functions as a declaration of allegiance and a yearning for transformation, expressing a desire that God's perfect will— often inscrutable and challenging—be enacted in tangible ways amid the brokenness of human existence. This invocation reminds believers that their prayers are not passive appeals but active commitments, inviting God's restorative power to permeate every facet of life. Furthermore, it highlights the reciprocal nature of divine-human interaction: while God's kingdom is established by divine authority, it is also realized through human obedience and participation. Theologically, this portion of the prayer bridges the temporal and eternal, urging believers to live in hopeful anticipation and faithful response to God's reign.

The plea "Give us today our daily bread" thrusts the believer into the realm of dependence and trust, acknowledging human vulnerability while affirming God's providential care. This simple yet profound request carries theological implications regarding sustenance, provision, and human need. Bread, in the biblical context, symbolizes more than physical nourishment; it connotes life itself—the essentials that sustain body and spirit. Through this petition, prayer becomes an act of humility that recognizes humans as creatures utterly reliant on divine generosity each day. It carries a powerful countercultural message in a world frequently driven by accumulative greed or anxious striving, encouraging a posture of daily trust that God will provide what is necessary in the present moment. Theologically, this phrase anchors the believer's faith in God's ongoing involvement in the mundane realities of life, thus bridging the sacred and the ordinary. It also invites reflection on the spiritual nourishment offered by God, as Jesus later reveals Himself as "the bread of life," deepening the meaning of this petition as a metaphor for ultimate sustenance and wholeness found only in God.

Moving into the realm of forgiveness, "Forgive us our debts, as we also have forgiven our debtors," the prayer navigates the intricate terrain of human sin and grace. This dual focus—the request for God's mercy paired with a commitment to mercy toward others—encapsulates the heart of Christian ethical living and theological understanding of salvation. To ask for forgiveness is to acknowledge personal wrongdoing and the need for divine cleansing and restoration. Yet, by coupling this confession with a call to forgive others, the prayer emphasizes the interconnectedness of grace and our human relationships. It reflects Jesus' teaching that receiving God's forgiveness compels the believer to extend the same grace to others as an authentic mark of transformed living. Theologically, this mutual forgiveness embodies the radical love of the gospel, which breaks down barriers of enmity and nurtures reconciliation. It also highlights the covenantal nature of God's mercy—gratitude for pardon leads naturally to a heart willing to forgive, recognizing that justice and mercy coexist within God's character. This portion of the prayer deepens the believer's awareness that forgiveness is not a private transaction but a communal reality reflecting God's kingdom principles.

"Lead us not into temptation, but deliver us from the evil one" confronts the spiritual realities of trial, warfare, and protection. This petition touches on profound theological questions about the presence of evil in the world, human susceptibility to sin, and divine safeguarding. It acknowledges that believers exist in a hostile spiritual environment where temptations and the influence of evil forces threaten faithfulness and holiness. The prayer thus becomes a plea for God's guidance away from harmful enticements and for rescue from the power of evil. Theologically, this recognizes God's sovereignty not only over blessings but also over the spiritual battles that believers face daily. It does not suggest that God tempts humans to sin, but rather requests divine help to avoid paths leading to destruction, emphasizing human vulnerability and divine protection. This phrase encapsulates the reality of spiritual warfare, invoking God's deliverance as essential for perseverance. It calls for humility and vigilance, grounding the believer's reliance on God's strength in the ongoing confrontation with evil and temptation.

Ending with the implicit doxology, "For yours is the kingdom and the power and the glory forever," the prayer reaffirms the eternal sovereignty of God, tying together the entire supplication within a framework of worshipful confidence. Though this conclusion is not present in all manuscript traditions, its theological resonance endures. It proclaims ultimate trust in God's rule over all creation, His omnipotence in sustaining it, and His glory as the rightful center of all existence. Theologically, it encapsulates the essence of Christian hope—despite present trials and unanswered prayers, God reigns supreme and will accomplish His purposes eternally. This affirmation provides a grounding peace, an enduring perspective that transcends temporal concerns and situates the believer's prayers within God's eternal plan. It invites reflection on the cosmic scope of God's kingdom, inspiring awe and surrender even as believers articulate their petitions.

Taken as a whole, the Lord's Prayer serves as a microcosm of Christian spirituality, encapsulating the believer's comprehensive engagement with God in prayer. It weaves together elements of praise—acknowledging God's holy name and kingdom; petition—seeking daily provision and deliverance from evil; confession—requesting forgiveness while committing to forgiveness; and commitment—submitting to God's will and persevering in hope. This integrated structure demonstrates that prayer is not merely the expression of isolated desires or fears, but a holistic communion that encompasses the divine-human relationship in its fullness. Theologically, it echoes foundational biblical themes: God as loving Father, the call to holiness, the anticipation of God's kingdom, the reality of sin and grace, the presence of evil, and the assurance of divine power and glory. Each petition and doxology invites the believer into a rhythm of prayer that is at once penitential and hopeful, reverent and relational, spiritual and practical.

Furthermore, the Lord's Prayer serves as a model for ethical formation. Its theological depth educates the believer not only about how to pray but how to live. By connecting divine attributes and actions with human responsibilities—such as forgiving others and submitting to God's will— it frames prayer as transformational dialogue that transforms hearts and actions. The prayer recognizes that spirituality cannot be detached from morality and community; rather, they are intricately linked within the web of divine-human encounter. This synthesis shapes how the believer approaches daily challenges and relationships, resulting in a lived faith informed and sustained by prayerful dependence on God.

In the broader theological landscape, the Lord's Prayer encapsulates the tension between the "already" and the "not yet" of the kingdom of God. As believers pray "Your kingdom come," they acknowledge that while God reigns eternally, the fullness of His reign awaits consummation. This eschatological tension invites sustained hope and perseverance, recognizing that the world remains imperfect and that prayer is a mode of participation in God's redemptive plan. The prayer thus assumes a dynamic role, inviting believers into active engagement with history and destiny, rather than escapist spirituality. This realization renews the meaning of prayer as a living encounter with a God who is active in the world, calling His people to faithfulness amid uncertainty.

Moreover, the Lord's Prayer transcends denominational boundaries, bearing a universal theological significance within the Christian tradition. Its succinct yet profound structure affords it a unique place in liturgical worship, personal devotion, and communal prayer. This ubiquity reflects its theological capacity to speak broadly yet deeply, addressing the core concerns of humanity and divinity with equal eloquence. In this way, the prayer becomes a shared spiritual heritage binding diverse Christian communities across time and geography in a collective whisper to heaven.

The theological significance of the Lord's Prayer also lies in its capacity to form a template for intimacy with God that balances petition with praise, confession with hope, and surrender with faithful persistence. It invites believers into a posture of vulnerable authenticity before a compassionate yet holy God. It encapsulates the paradox of Christian communion: a bold approach coupled with reverence, and confident requests tempered by submission to the divine will. This nuanced posture prevents prayer from becoming a shallow exercise or a manipulative demand, instead cultivating a sacred space where encounter with God nurtures transformation, peace, and empowerment.

Finally, contemplating the Lord's Prayer theologically reveals prayer itself as a sacred act that transcends mere words or ritual. It is a lived experience of entering into the mystery of God's presence, a means by which the believer's heart aligns with divine purposes, and a source of spiritual renewal and strength amid life's complexities. The prayer embodies the ongoing dialogue between human yearning and divine grace, revealing prayer as an ever-deepening communion that shapes identity, sustains hope, and nurtures the soul's whisper to heaven. In embracing the theological richness of this prayer, believers are invited to renew their own approach to prayer—moving beyond formulaic recitation into a vibrant, heartfelt conversation with the Living God, one that reflects the fullness of their faith journey and unfolds into transformation and sustained devotion.

Applying the Lord's Prayer

The Lord's Prayer, gifted to the world through the teachings of Jesus, stands as a profound and enduring exemplar of prayer, weaving together praise, petition, confession, and commitment in a seamless tapestry of spiritual conversation. Its structure reflects a divine rhythm that invites believers not only to recite words but to internalize a holistic approach to communion with God. When we engage with this prayer deeply, it becomes more than a ritual or familiar refrain; it transforms into a living guide that shapes our own language of prayer, informing and enriching the ways we speak to heaven.

To begin, the Lord's Prayer opens with adoration, immediately directing the heart's focus to God's supreme holiness and sovereignty: "Our Father in heaven, hallowed be your name." This is not a mere formality but a powerful invocation that realigns our perspective. It reminds us that prayer is born from a relationship with a loving Father, an intimate address that breaks down barriers of distance and formality while acknowledging divine transcendence. This balance is crucial. When we apply this opening invocation to our personal prayers, we are invited to pause and consciously lift God's name above all else—recognizing His sanctity, majesty, and the vastness of His presence. It challenges us to begin our prayers not with a wish list or hurried requests, but with an intentional moment of worship, where our souls are attuned to the sacred reality of who God is. In our own prayers, we are called to make space for this reverent praise, acknowledging God's holiness as the foundation of all that follows.

The petition that follows, "Your kingdom come, your will be done, on earth as it is in heaven," shifts the focus from God's transcendence to His immanent rule in the world and within our individual lives. This plea shapes the posture of all subsequent prayers, reminding us that our desires are ultimately aligned with God's greater plan, a divine will that transcends human understanding yet invites our participation. Applying this to personal prayer invites a humility that tempers our ambitions and fears, encouraging us to seek God's guidance and governance in every aspect of life. The Lord's Prayer models a prayer of submission, a surrender to divine authority that reshapes our will to harmonize with God's. Here lies an invitation to wrestle with the tension between our needs and God's perfect purposes, to bring our fragile hopes and fears into the sacred dialogue, trusting that God's will, though mysterious, is always life-giving. When adopting this posture personally, one cultivates an attitude of openness and trust, learning to listen and yield in prayer rather than merely speaking.

Further into the prayer, the focus moves toward tangible human needs with the petition, "Give us this day our daily bread." This plea grounds prayer in the reality of everyday dependence on God's provision. It doesn't ask for endless abundance but humbly requests sustenance sufficient for the day. This teaches us an essential lesson about the nature of prayer as a medium of reliance on God's faithfulness moment by moment. Incorporating this into personal prayer fosters a trust that is both practical and spiritual—a reliance not on future securities or material wealth, but on God's ongoing care and provision. This particular thread in the Lord's Prayer invites us to confront our anxieties and cultivate contentment, reminding us to return daily to God with our needs, trusting in His timing and grace. It offers a model for prayer that is neither rushed nor demanding but patient and steadfast, marked by a gentle expectation that God will provide what is truly necessary.

Another vital dimension in the Lord's Prayer is the confession that emerges as we say, "Forgive us our debts, as we also have forgiven our debtors." This mutuality of confession and forgiveness is deeply humbling and profoundly relational. It confronts us with the reality of our own brokenness and the imperative to extend grace to others. When weaving this into personal prayer, it compels us to examine our hearts honestly—to bring before God the weight of our shortcomings, while simultaneously cultivating a spirit of mercy towards those who have wronged us. This part of the prayer is neither easy nor superficial; it calls us into the painful yet liberating truth that forgiveness is the currency of the kingdom, a vital practice that frees both the forgiven and the forgiver. Applying this personally means allowing prayer to become a space for repentance and healing, fostering reconciliation not only vertically with God but horizontally with our fellow human beings. It reshapes our understanding of prayer into an active engagement with mercy, vulnerability, and transformation.

The Lord's Prayer culminates with a fervent plea for spiritual protection: "And lead us not into temptation, but deliver us from the evil one." This closing petition acknowledges the spiritual realities that surround us—the presence of temptation and the forces opposed to God's kingdom. It invites us to seek God's shelter and strength to navigate the trials and moral challenges that threaten our faith and integrity. When applied in personal prayer, this aspect teaches us the vital importance of spiritual vigilance and dependency on divine guidance in moments of weakness or uncertainty. It encourages a humble recognition of our limitations and the power of grace to sustain us. This portion of the prayer transforms our private conversations into a conscious fortification against the struggles within and without, turning prayer into a refuge and a source of courage. It also invites reflection on the multifaceted nature of evil, including doubt, despair, injustice, and sin, and urges us to rise above through resolute faith grounded in God's deliverance.

Embedded within these petitions and acknowledgments is an unspoken but powerful commitment: the alignment of our lives with God's purposes, a willingness to be formed by the words we pray. When personalizing the Lord's Prayer, it becomes more than a formula; it becomes a rhythm for living. Each line offers a spiritual exercise, inviting repeated meditation and incorporation into the flow of daily life. By returning to this prayer regularly, we allow its themes to sink deeply into our hearts, shaping not only how we pray but how we respond to the world. Its language forms a lens through which we view our challenges, joys, relationships, and inner struggles, providing a sacred perspective that sustains lifelong faith.

To apply the Lord's Prayer in a meaningful and personal way requires intentional reflection and a willingness to enter into its poetic simplicity without rushing for quick answers or superficial recitations. It asks us to dwell with the sacred pronouns—"Our Father," "us," "our debts"—reminding us that prayer is never solitary but part of a communal fabric. We pray as members of a larger body, connected by shared vulnerabilities and hopes, joined in a collective plea for God's kingdom and grace. This communal dimension enriches personal prayer with purpose and connection, fostering a spirituality that transcends isolation and self-centeredness.

Moreover, the Lord's Prayer invites an active listening alongside speaking. The rhythms of its sacred prose mimic the ebb and flow of intimate conversation, an ongoing dialogue rather than a monologue. Applying it personally means recognizing moments of silence, surrender, and waiting within prayer. It encourages us to respond to God's "hallowed be your name" with awe, to receive "daily bread" with gratitude, to enter into the tension of forgiveness with openness, and to cling to the plea for deliverance with steadfast hope. In doing so, prayer becomes a transformative means through which we are shaped from the inside out, molded by divine encounter and relational depth.

In practice, individuals can draw on the Lord's Prayer as a flexible template, allowing each line to inspire spontaneous and heartfelt expansions. It can guide prayers of quiet meditation upon waking, honest confession and petition during challenging times, or vibrant praise at moments of spiritual renewal. Each verse can become a seed planted in our hearts from which grows a rich and varied garden of personal prayers that reflect our unique life experiences while remaining rooted in the biblical tradition. This dynamic interplay between form and freedom keeps prayer alive and fresh, preventing it from becoming mechanical or rote.

Additionally, employing the Lord's Prayer as a model nurtures a balance that many struggle to achieve in their own prayers: the harmony between reverence and intimacy, humility and boldness, sorrow and hope. This balancing act reflects the complexity of human life itself, a complexity that prayer encapsulates beautifully. As we imitate this pattern, our prayers gain depth and authenticity, becoming expressions not of religious duty but of genuine communion, marked by trust and vulnerability. The Lord's Prayer thereby stands as a beacon, reminding us that prayer is not about perfection but about presence—a presence that honors God's holiness while embracing human frailty.

Finally, in embracing the Lord's Prayer as a personal tool, we join a timeless chorus of voices—from ancient followers of Jesus to modern believers—united in the sacred act of turning inward to God. This shared language knits together hearts across centuries and cultures, reminding us that our private prayers resonate within the eternal kingdom. Applying the Lord's Prayer personally opens us to a deep wellspring of spiritual strength and connection, beckoning us beyond our own concerns into a profound fellowship with the divine and with one another. It invites us to carry the prayer's sacred cadence into our daily lives, allowing our whispers to heaven to be shaped and guided by the transformative example left by Jesus, whose words continue to echo through the corridors of time, inviting all who listen into the mystery and power of prayer.